Praise for 7 Ste[illegible]

7 Steps to Success *is a must-read for all o*[illegible]*s out a clear path for success and provides guidance in making* [illegible]*. As a former major league baseball player, I witnessed many great athletes that would have benefitted tremendously from* 7 Steps.

Rick Ankiel
St. Louis Cardinals

In 2013, a father-daughter dream team, determined to make a difference in the lives of future generations, planted a seed that would become what is known today as Student ACES. This 501(c)(3) organization is dedicated to inspiring every student to achieve a foundation of honor, character and integrity that will leave a positive and permanent impression on their teams, schools and communities. What started as a dream with just 32 students has, in just a few years, grown to become a world-class organization that has served more than 24,000 high school student athletes to date. Buck Martinez is that father — and not just to his birth children; he is a father figure to all 24,000+ Student ACES. His passion, genuine goodwill and innate ability to connect with future generations and command their attention will forever go unrivaled in my eyes. I highly encourage anyone with children and everyone who works in a team environment to read the words of Buck Martinez – they serve as a reinforcement of just what it takes to be a leader in this journey we call life.

Jamie Levin
TBC Corporation
Student ACES Board Member

As a high school superintendent, I have the opportunity to witness so many young men and women who, with the proper guidance, could have identified and chosen the right path. Our young adults need a roadmap and 7 Steps to Success *provides clear guidance and direction. I encourage everyone to read this book.*

Angela Moore
Instructional Supervisor
Palm Beach County

7 Steps to Success *is a concise, on-point guide that speaks directly to the day-to-day issues facing youths, and how to be successful regardless of where you come from, who your parents are, and what you are individually going through. A must-*

read for anyone who wants the guidance needed to overcome life difficulties and succeed anyway.

LaVonne Idlette
Olympian, Serial Entrepreneur

As the CEO of a successful and growing healthy restaurant business, we aspire to have strong character and values from all of our team members. 7 Steps to Success *provides a clear and direct path for young adults to succeed in their respective endeavors. I applaud the guidance this book provides and will make it a must-read for all our team members.*

Chris Gannon
CEO, Bolay Restaurants

Buck knows what it takes to be successful in all areas of life – in career, in relationships, and balancing those with physical and spiritual wellness. He also has extensive experience conveying his recipe for success through his many years of leadership of Student ACES. The evidence is in the vast number of young leaders he has cultivated. He is an ideal author for a book on this topic!

Dr. Jennifer Sinclair Curtis
Dean, College of Engineering
University of California, Davis

Very seldom in one's life does one come to know a person who is 100 percent dedicated to helping youth of high school age become all they can be. Buck Martinez is that person. There are over 27,500 male and female student athletes that can attest to the value of knowing Buck and learning from him. He had designed all his past books, including this latest one, to provide detailed road maps of how to learn, live, and practice the values so essential to a successful and wonderful life. He teaches students how to overcome adversity and become leaders to train others. When it come to working with student athletes, Buck is the real deal.

Lieutenant General (retired) Robert Chelberg

As principal of an all-boys, college preparatory high school with the responsibility of guiding students to be productive members of society, I appreciate all the effort and dedication that Buck Martinez puts forth to motivate young men. He understands the difficult challenges that face our youth today and is passionately working to make a difference. Buck inspires us all by accepting the responsibility of leading by example and challenging young men to live a life of honor and integrity. His 7 Steps to Success *emphasizes the importance of the hard work, determination, and motivation necessary to achieve goals. Buck Martinez offers meaningful and insightful advice and encourages us to define our skills, enhance our values, and promote good decisions.*

David Pugh
Principal, Christopher Columbus High School (Miami, FL)

As a former professional athlete and a CEO of a very successful real estate development business, I have had the opportunity to coach and work with many people. 7 Steps to Success *provides a clear roadmap to young adults and young professionals in all walks of life to pursue and achieve a successful future. This book is a must read for those that aspire to greatness.*

Syd Kitson
CEO, Babcock Ranch

Unfortunately, many, who are trying to climb the ladder of success, realize too late that they've leaned their ladder up against the wrong building. 7 Steps to Success *not only gives you the "how to's" to succeed, and it also points you toward the right building on which to lean your ladder.*

George McGovern
Chaplain, New York Yankees

As the President of St. Thomas University and a former collegiate football coach, I believe it is of paramount importance to teach young adults about the values and guiding principles necessary for success. 7 Steps to Success *provides outstanding counsel for aspiring to greatness and following a pathway for success. I am excited about incorporating this book into our curriculum. The greatest compliment I can give to anyone is that they not only talk the talk, but they most certainly walk the walk. Buck Martinez is a great example of a St. Thomas University alumnus who is walking the walk by saving lives and transforming lives for the better of our society. We are very excited to partner with Buck to continue our mission to educate Leaders for Life at Saint Thomas University.*

David Armstrong
President, St. Thomas University

As a captain and a Hall of Famer at the collegiate and professional level, I understand what it takes to achieve success. The same mindset that allowed me to excel on the athletic fields has enabled me to develop a very successful construction business. I am thrilled that Buck has captured many of the principles that I followed in his new book, 7 Steps to Success for Young Adults. *I highly recommend this must read for all future leaders.*

Dwight Stephenson
NFL Hall of Famer
President, D. Stephenson Construction

Buck Martinez lays out the most important tactics for a person to succeed on purpose.

Congressman Brian Mast
Representative, 18th Congressional District, Florida

ACE is the place where the helpful mentors teach! Three years ago, I was invited to an event that was going to teach leadership skills to a couple of our students. Within the first few minutes of sitting in the back of the room listening to the presentation, I realized what my own next chapter was. As I look back over my career now, I realize that some of my best friends are individuals that I competed with daily. No, not anyone on the defensive side of the ball or in any other positions; the guys in my position (Running Back) who were some of the ones I was closest to. That's because of a saying my dad used to declare, "iron sharpens iron." He would tell me to stay sharp and HELP SHARPEN OTHERS! That's what I did in my career, and that's what I do through and with the Student ACES program as the Head Coach. Buck and Krissy are some of the sharpest people I know. Every day they are doing everything in their power to reach as many kids as possible. Since aligning with the Student ACES program, I have become a better person and mentor. Buck has taken me under his wing and personally coached me on reaching even those young people who are deemed unreachable. What the ACES program stands for is incredible. Do the right thing, the right way, as much as possible, and success will find you. This is one of the quotes from Buck that resonates in my soul. The passion he displays for leadership, as well as the guidance he gives about attitude, is what makes him and his team the leaders in the industry. I only hope that I can continue to align and sharpen myself with Buck, Student ACES and family.

Head Coach Donnell Bennett, Jr.

Praise for Man Up

Being a "Good Man" gets harder and harder in our time as our culture confuses what that means. Buck Martinez provides us, especially millennials, what we should expect of our sons – and ourselves.

Congressman Tom Rooney
United States Representative
Florida District 17

It is my honor and pleasure to recommend and encourage everyone to read Man Up. It's time for ALL men to "Man Up" so they can fulfill their God-given roles and assume their rightful place in our society. Recently I participated in Buck Martinez's ACE Leadership Summit for 175 Team Captains in Broward County, Florida and witnessed first-hand the commitment and compassion that he has to restore men to their rightful and God ordained place in the home, the workplace, the church, and the community. Buck believes that it's time to turn the clock back to the time when men were seen as strong, hardworking, loving husbands and fathers and I believe that this book could help us get there.

Coach Mike Jarvis
Head Coach, Men's Basketball
Florida Atlantic University

Buck Martinez offers definitive thoughts about man and his role in society. He identifies and explains some critical qualities that can help young men grow into meaningful adults. The wisdom and insights included can help readers young and old, maneuver life's journey today and tomorrow.

Romeo Crennel
Defensive Coordinator and Assistant Head Coach
Houston Texans

Man Up *is full of hope for the children of our future and gives a vibrant understanding of the importance of having a father who is committed to his family and community. While Buck's glass is almost always half-full, mine, as I read this book, brims over.*

Chris Gannon
CEO Bolay, and father of two

Praise for Straight Talk

Straight Talk *will be my go-to guide to get me through college and beyond. Finally, a resource for young adults that doesn't beat around the bush or sugar-coat the challenging aspects of life! In a society where so many people are concerned about the feelings of others, important life messages are often lost or glazed over. This book perfectly highlights those crucial messages.* ***Straight Talk*** *gives me the confidence of knowing what is to come and how to handle difficult situations and adversity. Thank you, Buck, for preparing me and my generation, so we can excel as the next generation of leaders.*

Rebecca Tucker
Student, University of South Carolina

Buck has done a magnificent job at addressing today's real issues for our youth. Young men and women are yearning for this dialogue, but all too often, don't find the wise counsel they are looking for by those around them. I highly encourage this book as a practical application for wherever you find yourself and your current season of life. Teenagers, young adults and young professionals can all benefit from Straight Talk!

Chad Jenkins
Jenkins Group

One of the more painful regrets in life comes from an individual not reaching their maximum potential due to decisions made in their nonage. In writing Straight Talk, Buck Martinez provides the wake-up call to young adults everywhere, and provides solutions to questions that are not always covered in the classroom or at home.

Tre Gabriel
Student and Football Player, Columbia University

Also by Buck Martinez

Building Blocks of Leadership for Young Adults

Captains Playbook: A Guide for Being a Leader On and Off the Field

Straight Talk: An honest conversation tackling the difficult issues facing our young leaders

Man Up: Leading a Life of Honor

7 STEPS TO SUCCESS FOR YOUNG ADULTS

BUCK MARTINEZ

ACE Leadership Group
Palm Beach Gardens

ISBN: 978-0-9976415-2-3
Published by ACE Leadership Group
Palm Beach Gardens, FL 850-559-7612
www.studentacesforleadership.com

Table of Contents

A Tribute

As *7 Steps to Success* was being published, we learned of the tragic and untimely death of Kobe Bryant and his daughter Gianna. Kobe exemplified many of the principles in this book, most notably "Winning Attitude" and "Outworking Everyone Else."

I have referenced Kobe in my work on many occasions as he was an individual that was the consummate competitor, a real-life warrior. He understood the concept of always being prepared and he never let anyone outwork him. Kobe represented all of his Laker and Olympic teams with honor. Kobe's winning attitude went far beyond the basketball court. He was a terrific husband, father, businessman and coach to his children. Even though Kobe experienced tremendous success, he also dealt with adversity on and off the court. His perseverance, determination and relentless pursuit to be the best at everything he did was something I admired and marveled at.

One of his quotes made such a lasting impression on me because it captured the essence of who he was, and why he did what he did, "God gave me talent, but I always worked as if I had none."

Rest in peace Kobe, you will be missed!

Foreword by Coach Paul Manieri

AS A YOUNG ADULT, YOU HAVE your entire life ahead of you. The decisions you make will have a significant impact on your success. As a father, grandfather, teacher, and lifelong coach, I have spent my entire professional life working with young men and women. One of my true passions in life is teaching values that will help young men and women develop into successful persons and become the future leaders of our country.

This book is intended to provide our future leaders with a roadmap to success. Each of our young men and women will face challenges and will deal with adversity throughout their life. We cannot control when or where we face adversity, yet there are lessons that can be taught to help young people overcome adversity and succeed in life.

Being a young adult today is very difficult. Although our schools do their best to prepare our students with the required knowledge, we mostly learn life skills through life experiences. Parents have a huge responsibility to teach their children skills that will help them, but unfortunately, many parents fail to do so for a number of reasons:

- They are a single parent and working multiple jobs
- They expect the school system to carry the load

- They have broken homes
- They do not care
- They assume that somebody else will do it

As a young adult, you can unknowingly make mistakes that will hurt you throughout your entire life, and in some cases, you will not have a chance to redeem yourself.

In my coaching profession, I have had the opportunity to work with some of the best colleges in the country, the U.S. Air Force Academy, St. Thomas University, Notre Dame, and my current school, Louisiana State University. I have also had the fortune of coaching Team USA. At each of the universities and at Team USA I have had wonderful experiences working with student athletes, many of whom have made it to the major leagues or are now coaching in their own collegiate setting. I believe all my experiences have provided a deep insight into how success can be pursued and attained.

7 Steps to Success provides a roadmap for success. It is my sincere desire is that this book guide you and provide you with valuable insight in achieving your desired path. Take the time to read thoroughly and be willing to discuss with your parents, your friends and your fellow students or workers.

I wish you the best in all of your future endeavors.

Coach Paul Mainieri

Chapter 1 – Develop and Maintain a Winning Attitude

IF YOU ASK PEOPLE TO DEFINE ATTITUDE, you end up with many different answers. Attitude is intangible so it is difficult to measure. Attitude is the lens through how you see life. Many factors affect your attitude, and one of the most important is the behaviors that you observe in your parents, teachers, coaches and other influential persons in your upbringing. What you observe from your parents is critical: how they act, how they approach things and how they address adversity. The same applies to coaches and teachers. Imagine playing for a coach who has a negative attitude and doesn't instill confidence in the team. If you have been in this situation, you understand that a coach's attitude can make or break a team. A teacher that doesn't instill a can-do attitude in students is dishonorable. Teachers can have a tremendous impact on their students. Those who fail to inspire and portray winning attitudes should not be in the profession. It is an honor to be able to teach others. If your heart isn't in it, you are doing a tremendous disservice to others.

Another important factor in developing a positive attitude is developing good habits. If you develop good habits such as working hard, being self-disciplined, studying hard, and being honest, you will have success. Experiencing success is a good way to develop a positive attitude because you will become experienced in the right behaviors. You can develop good habits by observing people you respect. Identify people worthy of your respect because they are honorable and demonstrate sound leadership. People are often attracted to individuals who are popular but do not espouse the values that drive success. Focus on traits you believe contribute to a winning attitude.

When you repeatedly do the right thing, you learn good judgment. The ability to understand right from wrong and the ability to make good decisions is important in developing a winning attitude. Let's look at the most important steps in developing a winning attitude.

Think positively

Winners must be capable of having a positive outlook. Winners understand that adversity is part of life -- there are ups and downs. More importantly, they understand that long term success is ultimately contingent on overcoming adversity. Winners view adversity as a challenge not as defeat. Winners remain positive and exude a positive demeanor to their colleagues, their teammates and to everyone they come in contact with.

Have a clear vision with measurable goals

Winners understand that they must have a clear vision and checkpoints to determine if they are headed in the right direction. Imagine playing in a big football game where the objective is to win, however, no one is keeping score. The teams would not be able to determine if they were on the right track with their vision. A similar analogy is planning a trip but failing to include check points to determine if you are heading in the right direction. Winners must understand that achieving their vision will require hurdles. Winners must ensure that they clearly communicate progress on their goals and must be able to address their hurdles with a positive attitude and a sense of confidence and determination.

Winners develop an unquenchable passion

Passion is one of my favorite words. Passion is the fire that burns inside of you and drives you toward fulfilling your vision. Passion is a critical element of a winning attitude. Think of passion as a flame lit inside of you and constantly being turned up as your passion intensifies. Winners must have a passion for what they do. They must be excited, determined, and relentless in the pursuit of their passion. Winners have amazing passion. They love what they do, they realize that there will be ups and downs, but their passion will not waiver. Passion is the difference between those who persevere and achieve their vision and those that fall short. Passion is the one thing that doesn't allow you to quit, it is the flame that doesn't burn out.

Entitlement will ensure failure

I am a big believer in working hard and being prepared as major factors in developing a winning attitude. If you approach your preparation for a big test, a big game, or a big presentation like you would for the actual event, you have a winning attitude. Everyone can get excited about the big event, but only winners practice with the same level of preparation and intensity. Many people today have an attitude of complacency. In too many cases, society rewards people for poor behavior. The term used today is "entitlement." This means that you have an attitude that you will be provided for even though you haven't earned something. Entitlement is disruptive and keeps people from striving to be the best that they can be. Over the past decade, our government has made it a habit to "bail out companies or industries that were not competitive." What message is that sending? I don't have to produce a better product or worry about keeping my costs competitive? The concept of rewarding mediocrity creates a workforce content with just getting by, not running to get ahead. You need to make sure that you conduct an attitude check periodically. Do you want to run ahead of the pack, or do you want to be middle of the road and pushing hard to get to the bottom? Entitlement creates losing attitudes and will keep you from achieving success.

Choose friends and associates that have winning attitudes

There is a saying that "You can't choose your family, but you can choose your friends." The meaning behind this is that sometimes people are not blessed with the best family, and their relationships suffer. Friends are the people you select to spend many hours and many days with. When you select your friends, you need to do a great job in screening to make sure they are the right fit for you. Each of us needs friends to share with, to laugh with and to cry with. Friends are your closest confidantes. Having the right friends with the right attitude will help you tremendously in life. You will be able to lean on them for support and guidance and they can do the same for you. Friends with the right attitude will help you develop and sustain the right attitude through life.

Perseverance

Perseverance is the determination that keeps us from quitting and keeps us fighting to accomplish our goals. Perseverance requires us to have a relentless commitment to our vision. Perseverance is also the engine that gets us back up every time life knocks us down. It keeps us from getting discouraged when someone rejects us or we have a temporary setback. Perseverance is the force that overcomes all the negative thoughts that enter our head. It allows us to filter the harsh criticism of our opponents and makes us more determined, more focused, and more aware of what we need to do to be better. Perseverance is one of the key ingredients of a winning attitude.

That which cannot destroy us makes us stronger

As a child we all heard the phrase, "If it doesn't kill you, it will make you stronger." The phrase was typically used as a joke when a child picked up a bug or something from the ground and placed it in their mouth. I see this all the time with my grandchildren; they will pick up random stuff off the ground and place it in their mouth. But behind the humor is a serious lesson.

A winning attitude requires that you push through the difficult times. That is what winners do. Whether it happens in school, in business, or in sports, you will experience setbacks. You could be blindsided by a test that you were not prepared for, or if you are in the business world you may lose one of your top clients; in sports, you always face the risk of injuries. Winners are capable of understanding this and recognize that these difficulties are a part of life. A winning attitude will not only get you through, it will make you stronger. This is what winners do. Keep your winning attitude on fire and let your setbacks make you stronger.

Good health generates positive energy

When we feel good our attitude reflects it. I am a firm believer that being physically fit is a key aspect of a winning attitude. When you are fit you have greater levels of energy and you feel good. It is important to be in good shape. It is important to eat right, exercise regularly, and get the proper amount of sleep. By doing this you will develop healthy habits which will contribute to your winning attitude. When you do not eat right or miss workouts, you feel sluggish and risk becoming temperamental. The same is true when you don't get proper rest. When you see people, and we all do, that look terrible and look miserable, it is typically that they have not slept enough. This can cause a negative attitude and can create hardships with people at school, work, or in your family. Winners need to pay attention to their health. A healthy profile will help develop and maintain a winning attitude.

Success is the best revenge

Each of you will deal with the difficult issue of jealousy and greed directed at you. There are people in this world who cannot accept someone else's success. Whether it is jealousy or greed, they will do their best to bad-mouth you, undermine you, or diminish your success. As a winner, you cannot let these petty issues get the best of you. Take the high road and show people that you are better than the selfish and insecure persons that attack you. Your competitive streak will always challenge you to go after the people that are doing you harm; however, revenge will hurt your winning attitude and cause you to become less of a person. Let your actions be your mouthpiece and rise above the nonsense. Your continued success is the best course for your revenge. Let whoever is cowardly and attacking you behind your back know that they cannot affect you, but you will become stronger and more motivated.

Preparation is an important element of a winning attitude

Being well prepared is an important piece of a winning attitude. By studying hard, you will always have the confidence that you will do well in your test. The same applies to working, sports, the arts, or any aspect of your life. By being prepared you will be able to handle any situation life throws at you. Being prepared keeps you from becoming rattled, especially, when you are confronted with difficult situations. Don't allow yourself to be caught unprepared; always think ahead and always anticipate your next move. Winning attitudes require that you are prepared and in control of the situation.

Why are you trying so hard to fit in, when you're born to stand out?

—Oliver James

Your Attitude will Drive your Success

I was in the corporate world for more than thirty years and I have observed how some people's careers have evolved and how others have imploded. I have seen brilliant Ivy Leaguers fail and I have seen individuals with less impressive degrees, or even no degree at all, have tremendous success. Through my years of observation, I came to the conclusion that the most powerful quality an individual possesses is their attitude. Unfortunately, attitude is not something that you can display on a résumé or a job application; even in job interviews, it is difficult to grasp a good perspective on someone's attitude.

The amazing thing about attitude is that you can't go to school to learn it, and you will not be able to purchase it at a store. All the money in the world will not buy you a winning attitude. A winning attitude is something that comes from within. It is the force that that helps you see things from a positive perspective. It is what defines winners and what separates winning and losing. A winning attitude is not something that you are born with. It requires your constant work and attention to develop it and maintain it. Sometimes it takes someone else to point out to us that our attitude needs work. When you develop a tight confidant or group of confidants that are willing and capable of providing you with candid feedback, you are a step ahead.

The quickest way of losing your job or getting demoted is to develop a negative attitude. People with negative attitudes are toxic and have the potential to bring the entire unit down with them. Sometimes negative attitudes can develop when someone faces adversity. Difficult situations such as an illness, the loss of a loved one, the loss of your job or other adversity, can challenge you and test your attitude. Do not let a negative attitude grow within and defeat you! Despite adversity, it is important to rise to the occasion and face your challenge. Doing it with a "can do" attitude and a positive frame of mind will help you and is critical to your success. Remember that each of us will face tremendous adversity in our lives, how someone deals with adversity separates those who will become successful from those who will not.

People with positive can-do attitudes produce winning results and will experience greater success in life. People with positive attitudes are successful in business, in sports, in family life and in social interactions. They demonstrate confidence and are eager to embrace life.

If you believe you can, you probably can. If you believe you won't, you most assuredly won't. Belief is the ignition switch that gets you off the launching pad.

– Dennis Whitley

Mo’ne Davis has a winning attitude

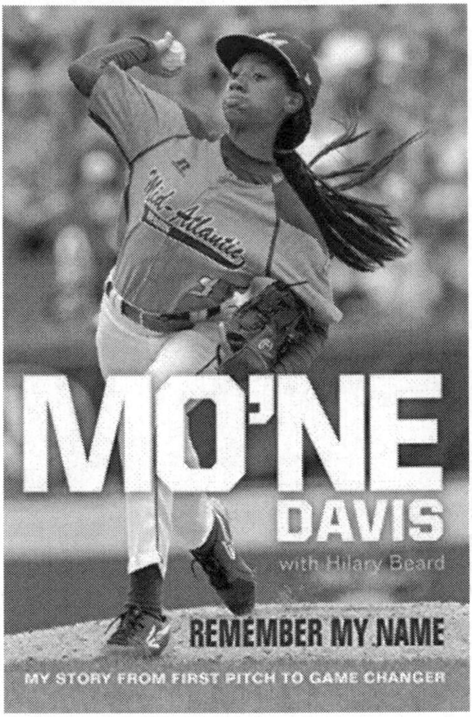

One of the most amazing stories of 2014 was that of Mo’ne Davis. Mo’ne was a thirteen-year-old girl who played baseball on an all-boys team -- she was the only girl on her team. What makes Mo’ne special is not that she played baseball, it is that she was a dominant player. She led her team to the Little League World Series and was absolutely spectacular. Mo’ne displayed a winning attitude throughout the Little League World Series. She was charming with the press and carried herself with the composure of a winner. I also admired how all the boys from her team and from the opposing teams admired her; not because she is a girl, but because she conducted herself with a winning attitude. Whether or not she makes it in baseball is irrelevant. She will be a tremendous success in life.

Before the Little League World Series, Philadelphia Magazine called Davis "the heart and soul of the team," complete with "long, flowing braids that cover the surname and numbers on the back of her uniform."

"She possessed incredible leadership, and you can't shake her; she's unflappable," Davis' coach, Alex Rice, told ESPN. "Hit a home run off her and she'll just give a little smile and get back to work. She doesn't get rattled."

Mo'ne has the attitude of a winner. She stands up to all challenges and accepts them all with a nice smile. It must also take tremendous courage to be the only girl playing in a boys sport. I am convinced that her attitude was the difference-maker in the success of her team. She is a terrific example of what you can do with a positive attitude. There is no mountain that you can't climb and no adversity that you can't overcome with a winning attitude.

Today. Mo'Ne remains active in sports. She played softball and basketball on her high school team and plans on playing collegiate basketball.

Do you have a winning attitude? Do you face adversity with confidence or with fear? Develop a positive attitude and you can face all your demons with confidence.

Attitude is infectious

Have you ever been around a person who has an infectious disease? Everyone is trying to avoid that person because they do not want to get sick. The opposite is true for people with winning attitudes; everyone wants to be with them. Having a winning attitude is magnetic. It attracts people to you and people want to be associated with a winner. Have you ever observed how people with winning attitudes just tend to light up a room when they come in? They always seem to focus on making others feel special and rarely place any emphasis on themselves. Do you know people like that?

There is a young lady in my high school leadership program, Student ACES, who exemplifies winning attitude. Her name is Becca Tucker and she is a recent graduate from Cardinal Newman High School in West Palm, Florida and earned her bachelor's degree at the University of South Carolina. Becca has recently become the first alumni hired by Student ACES as an employee, where she is already making a significant impact. As a freshman at South Carolina, she became involved in a leadership program and it didn't take her long to become the leader of the organization. What makes Becca special is her humility. She is the person that works behind the scenes to help everyone be better. She was involved in numerous activities at her high school and everyone recognizes her for her kindness and gentle spirit. Becca exemplifies what a winning attitude is. She has a "can-do attitude" and works to bring everyone together at her school. Becca has been instrumental in the success of the Student ACES program. She works diligently behind the scenes and eagerly volunteers for all activities that involve the betterment of others.

Most recently, she befriended a lady that is quadriplegic and helped raise money for her cause. I have never witnessed Becca seek personal fame; her intentions are pure, and her positive attitude flows out of her. What an amazing young woman!

Becca is the type of person that you want to be associated with. She brings out the best in people and selflessly gives herself up for others. She has a winner's attitude and is making a positive impact in our world.

I am always observing people's attitudes and most recently, I have been able to observe many student attitudes among those who participate in my Student ACES program. The following are some of the traits I observe that contribute to a winning attitude:

- You have to have a purpose
- You have to believe in yourself and your capabilities
- You need to place greater emphasis on helping others than on pleasing yourself
- You need to have a sense of humor
- You should not take yourself too seriously
- You need to recognize adversity and look forward to the challenge of overcoming it
- You must stay focused on your purpose

After reading this book, challenge yourself to follow these tips and you will see a significant improvement in your outlook towards life. You will quickly begin to attract people to you. Strive to have an infectious attitude and you will see noticeable changes in your life. I am convinced that people with winning attitudes do better at school, at their work and have a great relationship with their family.

Life is 10 percent what happens to you and 90 percent how you respond to it.

–Lou Holtz

People with winning attitudes intuitively will either become part of a winning organization or will likely lead an organization. If you think about it, everyone wants to play for a winner and everyone at work wants to be part of a great team. People with negative attitudes have a hard time attracting people to play on their team, work for their organization or socialize with them. It is not comfortable to be with a negative person. Negative people will always be a turn off. Their focus will always be self-centered and not on the betterment of the team.

Today, our society constantly inundates us with negative stories. With the internet and news stations that are streaming news twenty four hours a day, we find it difficult to escape from hearing negative stories. Unfortunately, all the great stories of people doing good deeds or heroic acts typically do not make it to the nightly news. Recently, the new media has flooded their outlets with stories of community violence such as Ferguson and Baltimore. It tears me up to see young men and women destroying their own neighborhoods. Regardless of how you feel about an issue, it does not give you the right to destroy someone else's property or to cause physical harm to another person.

A stunning photo by Bishop M. Cromartie during the Baltimore riots shows a young boy who, on his own, decided to offer water bottles to police officers.

Despite all the pain and violence, something good comes out of these adverse situations. I was so impressed by the photo of a young boy who despite all the violence around him, was handing out water bottles to the police officers. What an amazing heart this young boy has. As adults, we sometimes learn wonderful lessons from children. This young man has a winning attitude and a huge heart. His actions served as a positive example countering all the negative behaviors that were on display. After the boy's photo of generosity swept the nation, more people started helping the police officers, offering them pizzas and other items.

An Infectious Winning Attitude

This young boy's action is a perfect example of how an infectious attitude works. His act caused others to begin performing acts of kindness towards the officers. Just think about your own personal situations and how your behavior and attitude can help influence others to do the same. Every day you have tremendous opportunities to make a difference in someone's life with your infectious attitude. Whether you are at school, at work, at your sporting event or just hanging out with your family, you will have numerous interactions with people. In many cases there will be some that need a lift. They might be suffering from an illness, they might be struggling with self-esteem, they might be suffering from a personal relationship; you just never know. You have a unique opportunity to take advantage of the situation and bring a smile to someone's face. Take the opportunity and you will see that not only do you make someone else feel better, but you will feel better too. Let your attitude be infectious and lead with your actions. When you have a winning attitude, you will make a tremendous impact on others. Be willing to offer a smile or lend a helping hand. Don't be afraid to smile at someone. Try saying good morning to total strangers and witness how they react. Your willingness to do these things will be noticeable and will lead others to do it. Go ahead, try it!

Attitude is a Game Changer

The term "game changer" has many connotations. There have been books written with "Game Changer" as a title. There are companies with "Game Changer" in their name. As a matter of fact, my brother managed a company named Game Changer. In sports, the term describes a key play in the game that turns the momentum around and ultimately the outcome of the game. Try to think back to a special moment in a game when the announcer uses the phrase "game changer." In football it is pretty common for an announcer to describe a critical fumble or interception as a turning point in the game or a game-changing moment.

Attitudes are game changers. How many times have you witnessed a person or persons that are having a tough time or are in a bad mood for no good reason, and someone with a winning attitude and a big smile changes their mood and manner? I see it all the time. In the corporate world you have all kinds of attitudes. You have individuals who are always positive and have a bright outlook on life. You also have individuals that always want to rain on your parade. No matter what, they always have a negative perspective and tend to bring people down. You also have people that are totally unpredictable; one minute they are positive and the next minute they are negative. You never know what to expect. These are the people that are so tough to deal with and also cause others to have mixed reaction. How many times have you heard several people describe the same person differently? It all depends on the latest interaction that they had with that person. Someone might describe the person as a great guy and the other person might describe him as a total jerk.

You want to consistently have a winning attitude, so that everyone who meets you and works with you sees it, respects you, and describes you to others in positive terms.

People with winning attitudes can have amazing impacts on others. The great football coach, Bill Parcells, was notorious for trading for players that he felt would make a significant positive impact on his team. He picked them not because they had great skills, but because they were positive, mature, and would be able to set an example on the field and in the locker room.

Attitude can be the intangible difference between successful organizations and those that are either mediocre or fail. Having the personality to lead others to your desired result is a special quality. People are always observing you and if they see you remaining positive despite troubled times, they will follow you and respect you.

Would you rather have a leader that faces adversity with the confidence and determination to succeed, or the individual that is creating excuses for why they can't succeed? I have a tremendous admiration for military leaders. No matter what the odds are, they have to develop strategies that work. Their nation is depending on them. Failure cannot be an option.

Churchill: A leader with a winning attitude

One of the most impressive and successful leaders in history was Winston Churchill. He will always be associated with standing up to the Nazi regime at a time when Europe was falling rapidly to the German onslaught. Churchill became Prime Minister of England after World War II had begun. Contrary to his predecessor, who advocated a policy of giving concessions to Germany, Churchill steadfastly refused to surrender to the Germans. At a time when most Europeans were war-weary, Churchill helped inspire British resistance, especially during the difficult early days of the war when the British Commonwealth and Empire stood alone in its active opposition to Adolf Hitler. Churchill was an effective leader and an incredible speaker, who used powerful speeches designed to motivate and inspire the British people. He also used public radio to ensure that everyone could hear his voice.

Churchill truly recognized the threat from Nazi Germany, and he knew that if he didn't stop Germany's aggressive expansion, it would be too late for the rest of Europe. In a way, you can contrast what Churchill faced to today's ISIS. The ISIS aggression and brutality continues to spread throughout Europe, Asia, and Africa.

Our courageous military leaders have done an amazing job in taking the fight to ISIS and today we remain hopeful that ISIS will be defeated. Unfortunately, ISIS is not a country but an ideology. Ideologies are difficult to fight as they are rooted in hate, not territorial boundaries. Somebody in a position of leadership needs to have the courage to stand up to this evil and defeat it, and I believe our current administration is doing this. One of Churchill's greatest quotes was as follows; "You ask, what is our aim? I can answer in one word: It is victory, victory at all costs, victory in spite of all terror, victory, however long and hard the road may be; for without victory, there is no survival."

One of Churchill's best strategic moves was convincing United States President Franklin Roosevelt to provide war supplies, ammunition, guns, tanks and planes to the Allies, a program known as Lend-Lease, before the Americans even entered the war. Without support and resources from the Americans, England was doomed. German aircraft pounded the major cities with bombs nearly every night, and the British armed forces were running out of ammunition and supplies. The rate of survival for British pilots was minimal and morale was low. Though the future looked grim, Churchill did all he could to keep British spirits high. Just as Churchill had predicted all along, the road to victory in World War II was long and difficult. France fell to the Nazis in June 1940. After France fell to Germany, Churchill gave one of his most powerful speeches in which he convinced the British people that there would be no surrender from England. Here is an excerpt from his speech.

> *"Even though large tracts of Europe and many old and famous States have fallen or may fall*

> *into the grip of the Gestapo and all the odious apparatus of Nazi rule, we shall not flag or fail.*
>
> *We shall go on to the end, we shall fight in France,*
>
> *we shall fight on the seas and oceans,*
>
> *we shall fight with growing confidence and growing strength in the air, we shall defend our Island, whatever the cost may be,*
>
> *we shall fight on the beaches,*
>
> *we shall fight on the landing grounds,*
>
> *we shall fight in the fields and in the streets,*
>
> *we shall fight in the hills;*
>
> *we shall never surrender, and even if, which I do not for a moment believe, this Island or a large part of it were subjugated and starving, then our Empire beyond the seas, armed and guarded by the British Fleet, would carry on the struggle, until, in God's good time, the New World, with all its power and might, steps forth to the rescue and the liberation of the old."*

Churchill led Britain as Prime Minister until the Allies secured victory over Nazi Germany.

Churchill made very difficult decisions as Prime Minister. His courage and unwavering positive attitude allowed England to retain its independence. He was quite ahead of his time. Despite the number of casualties suffered by England, Churchill was relentless and focused. He earned the trust of his people and of the nation. Because of his winning attitude, Churchill was able to preserve England's autonomy and help save Europe.

Success is not final; failure is not fatal: it is the courage to continue that counts.

–Winston Churchill

Are you focused on the thorns or the roses?

Have you ever noticed how several people can look at the same object or situation and come to different conclusions? A good example is when people watch a movie and one person thinks it's a masterpiece and the other person thinks it is a bust. The same applies to people's attitudes. They might have the same job and one person is thankful to have work and a chance to grow and the other sees it as a dead end. The lens through which we see life is different for everyone – but we can choose what that lens focuses on: the good things or the bad.

There is a saying that "One man's trash is another man's treasure." A positive attitude allows you to see all the opportunities and upsides in life. It allows you to become appreciative of everything and every opportunity that life brings you. This is why two people coming out of the same poverty-ridden neighborhood with the same economic situation can view things completely differently. One decides to study hard, work hard, stay out of trouble, and hang out with the right people; the other decides to feel sorry for himself, begins to make excuses for why he can't succeed, hangs out with people with losing attitudes and drops out of school. We see this happen every day.

How we view life will drive our success. I find it appalling that there are people in this world that make a living by taking advantage of situations to create tension, divide people, and ultimately try to make themselves important. We see this most when there is a situation like Ferguson or like Baltimore. I don't need to mention names because we know and they know who they are, but people that are divisive on issues such as racism, abortion, gay rights and other creates a destructive environment. They instill attitudes that are negative and angry and, in many cases, accompanied by violence.

The destructive people are opportunists and while they portray what they are doing as an act of caring for the individual that was harmed, what they really are is self-serving vultures that feed off people and communities. They go from event to event spewing their acts of anger. Next time you see one of these individuals on television, do your research and find how much the news media is paying them to appear on their show. When they show up on a television show stirring up trouble, more people tune in and this helps the network's ratings. The whole purpose is for the person to sound important, and for the network to make money. Wouldn't it be great if these individuals actually tried to help in difficult situations, calm people down, speak of unity and coming together, and try to create pride in America? They create destructive attitudes and make money doing it. These actions are shameful and reckless.

The opposite of these charlatans are people that have a true desire to bring hope and comfort to difficult situations. They view difficult situations as opportunities to help the people affected. They deliver winning attitudes by encouraging people to work together, to help each other out and to put their interests second to the situation at hand. I have tremendous admiration for people who dedicate their lives to helping others and who bring a message of hope and promise; no matter how difficult the situation.

Franklin Graham spreads his winning attitude around the world

An individual who emulates the behavior that I am describing is Franklin Graham. Mr. Graham oversees an organization, Samaritan's Purse, dedicated to providing support and help to people all over the world. When disasters such as earthquakes, tsunamis, hurricanes, and other natural disasters occur, Samaritans Purse is typically the first organization that responds. They are also doing missions and feeding the poor all over the world. As opposed to seeking personal gain and opportunities by preaching hate, anger and divisiveness, Mr. Graham encourages unity and an attitude of optimism. Franklin Graham has devoted his life to meeting the needs of people around the world and proclaiming the Gospel of Jesus Christ. The elder son of Billy and Ruth Bell Graham, he has served as President and CEO of Samaritan's Purse since 1979 and as President and CEO of the Billy Graham Evangelistic Association since 2001.

Under his leadership, Samaritan's Purse has met the needs of poor, sick, and suffering people in more than 100 countries. As an evangelist for the Billy Graham Evangelistic Association, he has led crusades around the world.

To truly understand the amazing effort that Samaritans Purse takes on, I have listed some of the projects that they have been involved in:

- International Crisis Respond
- Operation Christmas Child
- The Greatest Journey
- US Disaster Relief
- World Medical Mission
- Greta Home and Academy
- Children's Heart Project

- Operation Heal our Patriots
- Children's Ministries
- Construction Projects
- Crisis and Disaster Response
- Feeding Programs
- Health and Medical Ministries
- Ebola Crisis in West Africa
- Nepal Earthquakes
- Human Trafficking
- Cyclone Pam Response

There are many other relief efforts that Samaritan's Purse is involved in. These are just a few organizations in which they have performed admirably and helped an enormous amount of people in need.

When there is a crisis situation, do you want to be associated with the people focused on the thorns or those who focus on the roses? Always bring your winning attitude to even the most distressing situations and you will see the positive influence that you will have on people. When people are hurting and they need hope and encouragement, be the one that they can count on.

Everyone has bad days, and everyone is faced with difficult situations. Sometimes it feels that the world is crashing down on you. As a young adult, you will experience adversity. Think of all the difficult decisions that you will face in your high school, college and early adult life. Let me help you:

- What electives should I take?
- Do I try out for a sport, am I good enough?
- Do I have the courage to go out with the person I think I like?
- Who should I hang out with?
- What college should I apply to?
- Which college should I attend?
- What major should I concentrate in?
- What clubs are right for me?
- What companies should I try to get an internship with?
- Am I ready for a relationship?
- Am I too young to get married?
- Do I live in a dorm or off-campus?
- Can I afford all the expenses that I am incurring?

All these decisions seem like they could be overwhelming, but trust me, if you think through each decision, evaluate all the pros and cons of each decision, and discuss your options with your parents and others you trust, you will succeed and make the right decision. If you have a winning attitude you will discover that you can tackle each decision as it comes, and you will be amazed at how much confidence you will build. No matter what life throws at you, a winning attitude is the secret to success. Something that works for me when I have some adversity is to think about all the people that have it way worse. I quickly realize that I am very lucky and should be extremely thankful for all the blessings that the Good Lord has showered me with. Next time you feel like you are having a bad day or are dealing with a very difficult issue, think of these examples:

- Children in a cancer ward
- Elderly people in a nursing home that do not have family members visit them
- Homeless people that might have been military heroes but are suffering from mental illness
- Wounded veterans
- Refugees in the Middle East whose homes have been wiped out by terrorists
- People that are lonely and in despair and have thoughts of suicide
- Unwanted babies or children with no one to love them

I could list more, but I want to provide a contrast to show how much worse it could be. Imagine if your winning attitude was able to help in any of these situations – what action could you take?

If you can keep a good attitude through a bad situation, you are a winner in life.

Winners Have Great Attitudes

Isn't it amazing when we hear stories of individuals that experience life threatening events that have a severe impact on their physical and mental state and yet they overcome their adversity to become an inspiration to others? As I mentioned earlier, I have a tremendous amount of respect and admiration for our soldiers. Sometimes we forget that our entire military is a volunteer unit. No one is asking these brave men and women to risk their lives to fight for our freedom. They leave the country they love, their families and the comfort of their home, to venture into a strange and foreign land where they encounter hostility, they do not speak or understand the language, and in some cases, they fight to help those that do not want them there.

The number of soldiers that are experiencing physical and emotional hardship is growing. As the number of military engagements increase, the likelihood is that the number of casualties and disabilities will continue to rise. Despite the hardship that these brave men and women endure, many of them are using their talents to make a difference in our communities. Their winning attitude is what makes them capable of becoming such inspirations to others. It takes a tremendous amount of character to be able to deal with the hardship of losing a limb, dealing with Post Traumatic Stress

Syndrome and the emotional and mental anguish of witnessing the horrors of war. These young men and women then have to make the difficult transition from soldier to civilian.

Bryan Anderson: A hero with a winning attitude

One amazing story of a Winning Attitude is that of Bryan Anderson. Bryan was a young man who decided to join the Army at the age of 19. Like many of you reading this book, Bryan spend his life immersed in sports. He was inducted into the Army on the day that America will never forget, September 11, 2001.

The boy who had not yet turned 20 spent seven hours in a bus full of strangers headed to basic training on that day that changed America. His nation's challenge had become his story. He was scared and confused, but also proud when the mood of the young men and women on that dark bus evolved into defiance.

Four years later, Anderson was on his back on a Baghdad sidewalk, with both legs and his left hand blown off when the truck he was driving hit an improvised explosive device. Frantic buddies saved his life. "My mom's going to kill me," he remembers thinking.

Bryan's story is similar to many other veterans -- their world is turned upside down in a matter of seconds. One minute you are a healthy and physically fit young person and the next minute you are helpless and know that your world will be changed forever.

After his recovery, Bryan became determined to use his adversity to teach others about his ordeal. Bryan could have allowed his adversity to overwhelm him and we would all understand. Fortunately, Bryan decided that the fullness of a man is not to be determined by his physical limitations, but by his spirit and his winning attitude. Anderson illustrated his beliefs in a recent speech to 275 people at Misericordia University in northeast Pennsylvania. Anderson says living in the moment became his recovery philosophy. He gives 30-40 speeches a year. He acted in the movie The Wrestler, appeared on the television series CSI New York and wrote a book, No Turning Back. He is the national spokesman for the veterans' aid group, USA Cares.

"Why settle for a normal life when you can have an extraordinary life?" he says. Although Anderson can command up to $10,000 per speech, he sometimes volunteers his time as he did in Dallas, Pennsylvania for a scholarship fund memorializing Army Lt. Michael Cleary, a local soldier killed in Iraq in 2005 at the age of 24.

"I never felt I was going to die," Anderson tells an audience of students and adults from surrounding communities. But four months into his recovery, he landed hard in his darkest moment: he was alone in the shower looking down at a legless torso and thinking he was half a person. He says music rescued him, especially the song "Survive" by a band called Rise Against, made up of his boyhood friends.

During his talks, Anderson admits that he is strangely drawn to the memory of the "awesome" sensation that the bomb sent through his body. He praises as "life givers" the dozens of physical and occupational therapy students he met with earlier in the day. Minus prosthetic legs, Anderson jumps off his wheelchair and quickly scoots to the edge of the stage, where he declares himself three feet tall. It is an invitation to see him wholly as he is.

Bryan Anderson's story is filled with patriotism, eagerness, adversity, despair, determination and now excitement and willingness to give back. A young man battling for his life defies all odds, faces the thought of suicide and overcomes his dark thoughts by looking past his limitations and beyond to a world that is full of hope. Anderson has tremendous courage and tremendous heart. The difference maker was when his winning attitude was able to take over and turned out to be stronger than his despair. He is now using his winning attitude to help others move forward and overcome their adversity. His winning attitude is an inspiration for all. He reminds us that life is a blessing and you should live it to its fullest. Despite his tragedy, he has persevered and is now a living testimony that a winning attitude can help you overcome and achieve.

Winners have winning attitudes. No matter what you are trying to accomplish in life, try to do it with a winning attitude. Every aspect of life requires the best in you. Whether it is your school, your work, sports, the arts, your social relationships and most importantly, your family, a winning attitude is the difference between your success and your failure. Do you think you could pass school with a lousy attitude? Imagine if getting up every morning to go to school was a major event; or if, you just didn't care if you passed or fail. That would be disappointing and tragic; a total waste of a mind. Compare the attitude of someone that doesn't care to someone that is excited to meet friends, learn, engage in school activities and capture the total experience of school. Who do you think is going to be successful? Who do you think people want to associate with? Who do you think will become a leader in life? The same applies to work. Having talent and being smart may get you a job but sustaining a job and rising to be the best in your profession requires a winning attitude. Winning attitudes are what motivates others. Winning attitudes attract clients and vendors to you because they know that you will be successful.

In sports, winners have great attitudes. They instill confidence in the other players and they motivate and inspire everyone on the team to perform to their highest level. I have always felt that in sports, the difference between winning and losing is attitude. Great attitudes are what create chemistry in and out of the locker room, instilling a confidence and an edge that your opponent will sense and become aware of. Each of you that have participated in sports knows what it means to play against an opponent that no matter how bad things are, just keeps coming at you. They are driven and remain positive throughout the entire game. People with that type of winning attitude begin to rub off on others and before you know it, the entire team is believing that they can win. These are the type of persons you want to associate with. They will stay positive and if they lose, you can be assured that they will come at you more determined than ever. This is what you want to strive to be. A person that is always competing, failing to give up, determined to give it your best until it is over. Winners never quit. People with winning attitudes make others quit.

When you have exhausted all possibilities, remember this - you haven't!

–Thomas Edison

Donnell Bennett: Your attitude allows you to reach great altitude

One of the greatest speeches I have heard is from Donnell Bennett. Donnell is a dear friend and I love him like a brother.

Donnell is blessed with tremendous athleticism. He played for the University of Miami Hurricanes national championship football team where he started as a running back. Donnell was the team captain and was one of the top draft picks in the NFL draft. He played eight years in the NFL. Football is what Donnell did, but it is not who he is. He is a tremendous human being. He has mentored many young men and women and is the Head Coach of the Student ACES program.

Donnell is also a tremendous husband and father and a man of deep faith. His attitude is contagious, and his smile is captivating. When asked how he is doing, he always replies with a booming voice, "tremendously blessed."

Donnell gives a speech where he addresses how attitude is what allows you to reach great altitude. He does an amazing job and I would highly encourage everyone to listen to his message. In his speech, Donnell correlates a winning attitude to the flight of life. He encourages student athletes to adopt winning attitudes and soar in every aspect of their life.

Chapter 2 – Be Responsible and Dependable

BECOMING A RESPONSIBLE AND DEPENDABLE PERSON is not something that happens overnight -- you have to work on it all the time. As a child, your parents begin to slowly give you opportunities to earn their trust. They might have asked you to take out the garbage on certain days of the week or they may have asked you to mow the grass. Your willingness and ability to perform those tasks determined if you earned additional trust, or if you would regress. Many parents trust their children to do well in school, a trust given and nurtured until your grades suffer. Try to think of all the conversations you have had with your parents through the years in which they offered a reward in return for good grades. If you received straight A's, they gave you some form of a gift. Your parents trusted you to do well, and you trusted that they would keep their promise of giving you a gift. If both sides kept their promise, then both sides would increase their trust in each other.

The same principles apply in every phase of life. Have you ever held a babysitting job? There is no greater responsibility than someone trusting you with the safety and well-being of their child. Babysitting requires parents to have full trust in the babysitter. They expect the babysitter to be someone who is dependable and responsible. There are many different things you must do before people will considered you to be a such a person. The good news is that when someone labels you responsible and dependable, the label sticks until you do something to change people's minds. There is no worse feeling than when someone you trust lets you down. Have you ever been let down? Have you ever let someone else down? Either scenario is very difficult. It hurts and it causes lots of tension.

I know a young man whose father recently let him down. It was very difficult for him. Young adults want to trust their parents, but when they let you down it causes tremendous pain and disappointment. In the case of this young man, his father had promised him, on three different occasions, that he was going to buy him a car for college. The young man was already away at school and made three individual trips of over five hundred miles to meet his father and buy his new car. On the last trip, his dad never bothered to show up. He said that he was too busy. Imagine how broken-hearted the young man was. His father let him down on three different instances. I do not know the father, but his behavior has severed their relationship. Responsibility and dependability are two words that do not characterize the father's actions. Sometimes the people who hurt us the most are those we trust the most.

To become successful, you must earn the reputation of being a responsible and dependable person. No matter how many times you want to tell people, "words will not carry any weight, it must be your actions," people still blindly follow empty words. How do we become a person that is responsible and dependable? The following are a few tips that will help you in this area.

Be on time

Being on time is one of the most important aspects of dependability and responsibility. Think of all the times that you needed to be somewhere on time. Did you make it on time? Did someone let you down and make you late? Being tardy can cause you serious problems in life. If you are late for a test, the teacher might not let you take it or might even flunk you. If you are late for your ballgame, your coach will likely bench you, or even suspend you. If you are late for a job interview, the chances are that you will not get the job. If you are late for your first date, you will likely not have a second date with the same person. If you are late for work, your boss might fire you. Some people try to dismiss tardiness as "being fashionably late." This is just a cop-out for irresponsibility. No game can start until the players and the referees are ready.

There are many critical positions that require tremendous precision, and no one can afford to trust them to irresponsible people. For example, flight controllers are responsible for keeping all airplanes flying in a timely, efficient and safe manner. If they are not dependable, they could be responsible for horrific accidents. Our military personnel depend on each other to be on a precise schedule. Any deviation from the plan can allow the enemy to defeat them. There are no possible excuses for tardiness in the military.

Be a person that is prompt. Always understand the situation that lies ahead and make the necessary adjustments to avoid being late. Being on time is a critical element to demonstrating that you are a person that is responsible and dependable. Bill Belichick, considered by many to be the greatest football coach ever, considers it late if his players do not show up at least fifteen minutes before practice or meetings.

Do what you say you are going to do

It is easy to say you are going to do something, but unfortunately, people fail to deliver on their commitments. This happens all the time in business and in everyday life. Most people genuinely intend to do what they say they are going to do. Unfortunately, things happen, people get distracted, interruptions occur, people overestimate what they can actually do, and then they fail to deliver. You will be tested in every walk of life. How you perform on the test will determine how other people perceive you. One of the greatest failures in life is when someone is counting on your word and you fail to do as promised. Just like responsibility and dependability, failing to deliver will have serious consequences. If you commit to get good grades and then you fail to study, develop bad habits and ultimately have a poor report card, you failed to deliver on your commitment. If your coaches tell you that you have to report to practice at a certain weight and you report 20 pounds overweight, you let your coach, your team and yourself down. If you promise your parents or your fiancée that you will stop drinking and then you miss an important event because you were drunk, you have failed to deliver.

Failing to act on your commitments is one of the biggest causes of broken friendships, severed relationships, family breakups, and ultimately failure in school or failure in your job. Everyone wants to work, be teammates, and be friends with people who are responsible and dependable. Be that person.

If you make a mistake, own up to it

Everyone makes mistakes; that is part of being human. Think of all the mistakes that you have made in your young life. If you are like me, you have made many. Mistakes allow us to learn and become better. If you do not learn from your mistakes, you will regress and continue to act with poor judgment. Learning from our mistakes and using them to improve is what helps us grow. Mistakes help us understand certain weaknesses and overcoming them makes us stronger.

To get honest and valuable feedback, it is important to have a person or persons that you can trust. These are people who can be comfortable in pointing out your mistakes and providing you candid feedback in order to help you grow – not to run you down. If you are not aware that you are acting in an inappropriate manner, you will continue to exercise poor judgment until someone points out the flaw.

Most scandals in life are the result of trying to cover up a mistake instead of the mistake itself. Political scandals seem to always get the most attention. Two of our presidents, two presidents, Richard Nixon and Bill Clinton, created two of the most prominent. Each of these presidents was involved in an unethical situation. In both cases, they decided to cover up the mistake instead of admitting the truth. In Nixon's case, he was impeached by Congress and ultimately resigned from office. President Clinton was also impeached by Congress and caused tremendous dishonor to the White House, but somehow was able to keep his job.

When you make a mistake, you may feel that it is the end of the world, but trust me, admitting you made an error and accepting the consequence is the better option. When you lie and try to cover up the mistake, it creates a snowball effect. As the snowball rolls downhill, it gets bigger and bigger until it eventually creates tremendous damage.

If you know that you can't deliver on a promise, let the other party know as soon as you can

We are always eager to please others. Sometimes in our eagerness, we overcommit and make promises we cannot keep. As a young adult, you want to do your best and it is easy to get caught up in the moment and promise to do something that you really won't be able to complete. Sometimes you have to remember that you have a busy schedule and your days get full very quickly. You tend to have a full schedule with school, sports, music and art, and sometimes work. I also encourage you to get involved in activities or organizations to help others. There are many great causes that need everyone's help. But all these commitments mean you will have limited time available for additional projects and events.

When someone asks you to make a commitment, a good personal policy is to reply with, "Let me check my schedule and get back to you." This will allow you to check the prior commitments on your calendar to make sure that you are not overcommitting. Once you promise to be somewhere or work on a project, other people will feel let down if you don't fulfil what you said you would do.

Letting someone down who is counting on you is difficult, and depending on your commitment, it can be heartbreaking. People depend on you and if you let them down, this behavior will affect your relationship.

If you commit to do something and later find out that you have promised to do something you cannot do, you must let that person know as soon as you have discovered it. When you promise to do something, you owe other people the respect to tell them you can't do it.

As you get older in life and become a parent, your commitments to your spouse and children are even more important. You must be very careful to keep your commitments to them. Your children count on you to help them with school, take them to their ballgames or recitals, and to be there on special occasions such as birthdays and holidays. One of the greatest disappointments for a child for a parent to let them down.

It is not too early to begin developing good habits now and to be a person who can be counted on to deliver on their commitments.

Be honest

Honesty is a critical element of being responsible and dependable. If you are not an honest person, others will not trust you and you will develop a bad reputation. People will not want to do business with you or be associated with you. Would you want to be associated with a dishonest person? Would you trust your money with a person who is not trustworthy? Would you play for a dishonest coach? Would you live with a person you cannot trust? I hope you answered no to each of those questions.

Dishonesty is one of the worst traits that you can have. If you are not honest, you need to immediately begin a program that will steer you towards honest behavior. Dishonest people might make money at the expense of others, but I believe that they live miserably, always afraid of being caught in their lies. If you are dishonest and take advantage of people, they will find ways to get even; they might even try to hurt you physically. If you are dishonest, you will find it very difficult to develop lasting relationships.

Be a person that is dependable and trustworthy. This will give you lasting relationships, you will feel good about yourself and you will become a great person.

Be a person of strong character; do not let others negatively influence you

Becoming a person that is responsible and dependable requires you to have a strong character. There will be many people over time who will try to influence you, and not always in a positive manner. Think of all the potentially negative distractions that you will have to deal with every day from others, television or social media. The distractions and the negative messaging are constant – people who have bad habits always seem to want to drag others into their bad behavior. Let me give you a few examples:

- Drinking irresponsibly
- Illegal drugs
- Purchasing items you really can't afford
- Irresponsible relationships
- Hanging out with the wrong crowd
- Uncontrollable gambling
- Laziness and poor work ethic

All these activities will jeopardize your relationships and your personal integrity – they will keep you from becoming a person who is responsible and dependable. School requirements are intense, and they command a tremendous amount of your time. The same applies to a job. Employers expect you to be on time, properly rested and with a good attitude. You should always avoid engaging in activities that create a distraction from your responsibilities and will jeopardize your behavior. It only takes one stupid act to ruin your character and reputation. Be responsible and smart and you will be rewarded.

Recognize that everyone is human and will make mistakes

As humans, we all make mistakes. This is something that you have to recognize as a critical element of being responsible and dependable. When you allow someone to represent you in any capacity, you are placing your reputation on the line. For example, if you agree to do a job for someone and you decide to send a replacement, your credibility is on the line. If your replacement does a good job, you will be fine. If he doesn't, it is your reputation that will suffer. You must always take into consideration that people will make mistakes. Some people may not have a good work ethic or be trustworthy. You must be aware of who you allow to speak and act for you. Always be extremely careful of how your dependability will be affected when someone else represents you.

You must also realize that you will likely make mistakes, some intentional and some not. You might oversleep on the day of a big test, or a Saturday morning practice. Things like this happen and you must be capable of admitting your mistakes and moving forward. Mistakes are a big part of life. How you deal with them will define your character. You can address them head on, or you can try to cover them up. It is your choice. To be responsible and dependable allows you only one option. Make the right call!

Learn to Be Trusted

Without trust, relationships cannot exist. Think of every relationship that you have established. Do you think that the relationship could exist if you didn't trust the other person? Trust is paramount for any relationship to prosper. A relationship between you and your parents that is not based on trust is doomed to failure. It cannot be sustained. Trust is based on years of predictable behavior. As a child you are born with a pure heart and you eagerly trust people. You assume that everyone is trustworthy, and you assume that people will always treat you fairly. When you look through those tiny little eyes at complete strangers and your little hands hold the hand of a complete stranger, you are at the mercy of the other person and you can only assume that they have your best interests at heart. It is not until you became cognizant of how others knowingly and willingly act that you can make your judgment.

Unfortunately, there are all types of people. Some are good natured and act in your best interest, and there are others who, either deliberately or not, will place their own interests first. Anything that conflicts with their interests will be compromised, including you. As a young adult you must develop a keen sense of awareness. You need to develop a relationship with someone before you decide to place your trust in them.

Recently we have learned of numerous scandals involving people who placed their life savings in the hands of a financial advisor, only to witness their entire life savings disappear into the hands of a corrupt individual. As a young adult you need to gain an education in how to manage your money. There are too many individuals who prey on those that have lots of money, but lack the knowledge or education to manage it.

We see this scenario play out a lot in sports. Many young athletes are rewarded handsomely by teams and corporate sponsorships for their athletic prowess, only to lose their wealth to sharks. In the NFL, the average career is somewhere between 3.3 and 3.8 years, in essence, not for long. Of those that do make it into the NFL for a few years, 80% are broke by the time they are twenty-eight years old. Sadly, many entrust all their money to agents or investors that carelessly blow it on poor investments or wasteful excesses, or even steal this money by finding ways to funnel it off. I can only imagine the anger, the disappointment and the shock and disbelief of learning that your entire sports career has been blown apart by a person you trusted and probably referred to as a friend.

In some cases, people spend many years working towards a retirement only to see their company go broke. You must diversify your portfolio (don't put all your money into one investment!) and are prudent with your career earnings. Just like there are many irreputable people, there are also many highly qualified and competent professionals who can be trusted. Be smart, be savvy, and do your homework. Managing your money should not be about friendships, but about finding and working with competent and experienced professionals.

You might think there are many rich people that made their millions by taking advantage of others, and there are. I believe that even though they might be rich, they have to be empty inside. These people cannot be happy with themselves. They live by taking advantage of others and by manipulating their way to financial wealth. For the most part, these people die lonely and miserable, or they end up devastated themselves. We see these people in the headlines every day for wrongful acts.

As I was writing this book, a scandal erupted in which wealthy Hollywood people were paying a third party "consultant" to get their children accepted into very desirable colleges and universities. Large sums of money were going to an individual who brokered undeserving high school students the opportunity to go to the school of their choice. These students were sometimes presented to the college as being worthy of sports scholarships for sports they did not even participate in! I do not know how long this practice has been going on, but it is morally and ethically corrupt. I can only wonder how many deserving students were denied the opportunity to go to the college or university that they had sacrificed so much for. Imagine working so hard for something you want just to have someone steal the opportunity from you. These parents were shameful to stoop so low to provide their children with something that they did not earn or deserve.

To be dependable and responsible, you must be trusted and you must surround yourselves with individuals that are also trusted. If you associate with dishonest people it will ultimately affect you.

For some people, the ends justify the means and they will do everything they can to lie, cheat and steal from others to make themselves wealthier and more powerful. For them, nothing is never enough. They leave a trail of people they have trampled on, taken advantage of, or financially devastated.

Do you want to be a trusted individual? Would you rather be a person that gets away with fraud and deceit to make yourself rich? What kind of values and character do you want to be known for?

To be successful, you have to be considered as a dependable and responsible person.

You do not want to be viewed this way!

Many different people, organizations and institutions communicate with us – and *at* us – every day, and an almost unlimited number of relationships affect us: emails, television commercials, internet advertisements, information from your teachers, and instructions and projects from the organization you work for. In a matter of nanoseconds, you need to make a rational decision about what you trust as a credible source and what to dismiss. It seems that everyone is selling you something. There are endless numbers of commercials and their only purpose is to sell you something. Today you need to assimilate a tremendous amount of information in a very short time.

But who do you trust and why do you trust them? The trust you bestow on another person is a tremendous honor, and that trust something people must earn from you. When I think about people that I trust, I have to do a thorough assessment. There are many factors to evaluate before I trust someone, including:

- Do I trust their judgment?
- Are their intentions pure?

- Do they have a hidden agenda?
- Do they keep their word?
- Are their actions consistent with their words?
- Are they someone I would want representing me?
- Will they have my back in a dispute?
- Will they bend the truth?
- Do they study hard?
- Do they work hard or take shortcuts?
- Do they act in the best interest of their friends; their families?
- If they were a teammate or a coworker, would they be team oriented or self-centered?

When you think of "trust," what are some examples that come to mind?

- The trust between a husband and wife
- The trust between a child and his/her parents
- The trust between an athlete and his/her coach
- The trust between a teacher and a student
- The trust between someone in danger and a police officer
- The trust between a church and their pastor or rabbi

- The trust between the people and the President of the United States
- The trust between a soldier and his/her commanding officer

Trust is earned by someone's actions taken over a long period of time. Take a minute to think of people you trust. Why do you trust that person? It is likely that the person you trust has been reliable, dependable, and available when you needed them. It is also likely that their behavior has been steady and predictable. In addition, it is likely that their values are aligned with yours.

Trust is something that takes many years to cultivate, and yet it can be broken in a nanosecond. Recently, I had the opportunity to speak to a group of high school students from an impoverished area. Each of them had faced tremendous adversity in their life and their trust had been routinely violated throughout their young lives. I asked each of them to write down the names of five people that they trusted. Sadly enough, there was not one male person on the entire list. The majority of the students were not able to even list five names, and they struggled to name just a few people. I felt terrible for them. Imagine growing up in a place where you do not trust anyone -- not your family, not your teachers, not your coaches, and not even your pastors. These young men and women had experienced terrible abuse in their lives. They are now skeptical of people and will always have a hard time trusting anyone. This will affect their future families, their coworkers, and their social interactions.

Trust is the glue that binds all of our relationships and the one thing that makes us all stronger. A trusting family is a beautiful thing to experience. The great sports teams always have a special relationship between the players, and between the players and the coaches. In my professional life I have had the opportunity to work with trusted individuals. Being able to trust your fellow workers is a game changer in how your company performs. That trust between coworkers allows you to place your entire focus on your competitor rather than having to worry about your own teammates.

Trust, if developed and leveraged, has the potential to create unparalleled success and prosperity in every dimension of life. Yet, it is the least understood, most neglected and most underestimated possibility of our time.

—Stephen Covey

Keep your Commitments

If you want to be viewed as a responsible and dependable person, you must keep your commitments. Throughout your life you will be involved in many interactions and will likely have many types of relationships. As I think back through my life, there are many relationships that I engaged in at work, in sports, with my family, and with people from my children's school or our church. Regardless of the interaction or relationships, keeping your commitments is critical to your ability to become a successful and dependable person.

By keeping your commitments, you will develop a reputation as a trusted individual of integrity who always delivers.

When you make a commitment, you need to understand that there is an expectation that you will fulfill your commitment. Something you might perceive as trivial could be very important to the person you made the commitment to. For example, let's assume that your neighbors asked you to let their dog out because they were going to be late coming home from work, and you forgot. When the neighbors got home they found that there was pee and poop all over their furniture. In your mind, taking the dog out might not have been a big deal, but to the person you made the commitment to, it resulted in a tremendous amount of damage. The upholstery on their furniture needs to be replaced and they had to spend the night cleaning the house. Do you think the relationship between the two parties suffered? Do you think that not keeping a commitment will hurt your reputation? You must always be cognizant of the other person's expectation when you make a commitment.

There are some important factors you need consider when making commitments:

- You have to assume that all commitments, no matter how trivial they may seem, are important

- When you commit to do something, there is an expectation that you will keep the commitment. If you fail to carry out your commitment, the bond is broken and you fail both yourself and the other person

- Be clear as to what you agree to and make sure that both parties have the same understanding of what is to be done, and when

- In an effort to please others, we sometimes make hasty commitments without truly understanding what we agreed to. This happens every day and it is the number one issue that affects relationships. It is important to take the time to understand what the other person is asking you to do before you rush into saying yes. Always saying yes without thinking it through or checking your other commitments can cause hardship and can result in a serious misunderstanding

- Develop a process to ensure that you are fully aware of all your commitments, and learn how to politely decline when you are unable to take on another one

- Everyone uses a different technique to manage their activities. Some people keep everything in their iPhone while others write everything down in a planner. Try a few different options until you develop a process that works for you and allows you to be effective. As your life becomes busier, there will be distractions that affect your best laid plans. It is important that when the unexpected happens, it doesn't keep you from fulfilling your commitments. Whether it is social, school, family or business, you cannot afford to fail on your commitments. People are counting on you

- If you can't keep your commitment you must notify the other person immediately

- Most people understand that there are times when things get in the way of commitments. People get sick, people get flat tires, or unexpected things such as serious car accidents make us late for appointments. I have always found that if you communicate with people on your hardship, they will understand. It might also provide them time to devise an alternative plan. What you can't afford to do is to miss the commitment without communicating.

- After you successfully fulfill your commitment, ask for feedback

- Asking for feedback will ensure that both of you have a common understanding on whether the commitment was performed to the satisfaction of both parties and will establish the framework for the next opportunity. If you are asked to perform a task, take the time to ask the other person to rate your performance. This will allow you to address things that were unsatisfactory and make the necessary improvements.

Unless a commitment is made, there are only promises and hopes; but no plans.

–Peter F. Drucker

All through your life you will be making commitments. Some will be financial, others will require your time, and others will be relational. Financial requirements typically involve a transaction. You purchase something and you have to pay for it. In some cases, your purchase is a long-term commitment and involves having to finance or borrow money. When you borrow money, the business or person loaning you the money expects that you will pay it back in a timely manner. If you do not, there will be significant consequences. Financial commitments seem simple but yet there are significant numbers of people whose cars are taken away because they defaulted on their car payments, or who lost their home because they did not make all their mortgage payments on time. Having a poor record of paying on time then gives you a poor rating on your credit report, which can prevent you from renting an apartment, getting a good rate on a mortgage, or borrowing money to start a business.

If you are not sure that you can afford something, do not buy it. Committing to something – like a financial contract – that you can't deliver on will get you in trouble and keep you from being successful.

Marriage is a lifetime commitment

The two most important commitments that you will make in life is when you decide to get married and when you become a parent. Marriage is a significant step in your life and requires deep thought and reflection. Marriage is a commitment to be with someone throughout both your lives, "in sickness and in health, 'til death do us part." These are the words spoken by the bride and groom at the wedding. The words are powerful and have a deep meaning. You are committing to love and protect the other person throughout life. Marriage is not an easy thing and, unfortunately, one out of two marriages now end in break up.

I firmly believe that many marriages fail because the parties do not take their commitment seriously. Like any relationship, marriages have ups and downs. It is not easy and requires sacrifice, trust and respect. I am very fortunate that I belong to a family that has many long and successful marriages. My parents were married almost 60 years until my father passed away, and my brother and I have each been married for over 39 years. I am extremely blessed to be married to a wonderful woman and we both share a deep commitment to each other, to our marriage, and to our families. You must understand that every marriage can expect to experience hardships, but like all commitments, you should not give up when things aren't going great. Fight through the tough times and in many cases the relationship will become stronger. Everything in life that you value should be worth fighting for.

As a boy, my dream was to be a professional baseball player. I had the talent and despite numerous injuries through high school, I was able to have a very successful college career. Many scouts told me that I had the talent to be a successful ballplayer, but the shoulder injuries had taken their toll. I graduated college with an unquenchable thirst to pursue a professional baseball career. I had never fully recovered from a serious shoulder injury, but I wanted to give professional baseball a shot. Unfortunately, I had already accepted an offer from an insurance firm, and I had committed to work for them for minimum of twelve months. I decided to try to get out of the commitment and spoke to my boss about my decision. Fortunately for me, he voided the one year commitment after I had spent six months on the job. His willingness to help me allowed me to train and prepare for a baseball tryout with the Cincinnati Reds.

This experience made me realize that it was immature for me to accept a one-year commitment without the mental readiness to stick with it. I felt bad about not keeping my commitment, but it was a valuable lesson in responsibility. You should always be aware of each and every commitment you are getting into, and you should never make any commitment until you are emotionally, mentally and physically prepared to carry it out. Your ability to become recognized as a person that keeps his/her commitments will create greater and greater opportunities for you and will earn you a wonderful reputation.

Commitment is an act, not a word.

–Jean-Paul Sartre

Develop and use great communication skills

Communication skills are very important in becoming a person that is dependable and responsible. We often assume that the person we're talking with has a good understanding of everything we said. Amazingly enough, poor communication is always the number one reason why relationships fail. This is why there are thousands of books on the subject. Over the years I have witnessed family disputes, failed business deals and the breakup of great sports teams because of a breakdown in communication. When you make a commitment, you must get a deep understanding of the other person's expectations. I have found that a good tool for checking that you both have the same understanding is to repeat what you heard back to the person. For example, "Just to be clear, I want to repeat back to you what I think I heard you say to be sure that I fully understand what you said." This is an effective way to confirm the understanding before you leave the conversation – it gives the other person the opportunity to confirm or correct what was said. I can cite numerous times when I have heard people say, "I heard what you said, but I thought you meant something different." According to a blog named Project Excellence, there is a fifty percent of failure in projects due to failed communication. According to this blog,"Ineffective communication is the primary contributor to project failure one third of the time, and had a negative impact on project success more than half the time."

Over the course of history, there have been numerous incidents where misunderstandings created tension between countries, breakups in business ventures, the dissolution of marriages, the collapse of sports dynasties, and the failure of partnerships between celebrities and their agents.

In 1998, NASA launched a spacecraft, the Mars Climate Orbiter, to study the critical elements of the Red Planet. No spacecraft had ever approached the mysterious planet at such a close proximity. For many years, scientists have been intrigued to learn whether or not life exists on Mars and this mission would help solve the riddle. The Mars Climate Orbiter would provide critical data on the temperature, the climate, and whether or not water is present in the Martian environment. The spacecraft was supposed to enter Mars' orbit at a specific altitude and position, giving it of margin for error. The minimum altitude the spacecraft needed to be safe was just 80 km. But the orbiter lost contact and was presumed destroyed before it ever collected any information. Based on what NASA could piece together, the contractor for the software giving instructions to the lander used a different unit of measurement than NASA had specified. Instead of using the requested measurement of newton-seconds, the contractor's software used pound-force seconds, putting the spacecraft in the wrong position in the atmosphere, where it disintegrated. The critical mission was lost and a tremendous amount of time, money and manpower was lost, and affected future aspects of the space program.

How could these brilliant scientists miss their target? Had there been clearer communication and goal alignment between the software provider and NASA, such a mundane unit conversion mistake could have been avoided and the $300 million space mission might have succeeded.

Every year we witness many tragedies resulting from a lack of communication. What we do not hear about are the number of near misses. Whether it is friendly fire, lack of understanding the cultural differences in other countries, or the egos that undermine what could be highly profitable business mergers, careful communication is typically the missing ingredient. How many times have we said things like, "What I thought you meant was…"

I always think about the great Los Angeles Lakers teams of Kobe and Shaq. Unfortunately for Laker fans, the dynamic duo's failure to communicate about their vision and their respective roles likely cost them the opportunity to win more NBA titles. The same situation applies to LeBron James and Kyrie Irving, who failed to develop the rapport and relationship that fans hoped for.

It is very important to understand the personalities involved when you are getting involved in a commitment. Despite what is committed to writing, people tend to interpret things according to how they want to see the outcome. Communication is paramount to a successful relationship and to how you manage that relationship.

Can you think of any relationship you are involved where improved communications can prevent a hardship?

Establish a network of trusted confidants

To become a responsible and dependable person you need to develop a network of trusted confidants. These are people you can count on when you need to get something done. These are also people who you know that if they told you it was going to get done, it will, regardless of the situation. As a dependable person it is important to understand that people will measure and assess you in part based on the people that you surround yourself with. There will be times when you must rely on your network of associates to fulfill an obligation. If your network is comprised of people who cannot be trusted, it will reflect on you. This applies to school, work, sports, and your social life.

In school you should always try to establish a group of trusted peers that will help make you greater. Try to create a network of individuals that will help each other and complement each other's skills. For example, would they be able to support a study group? Would they be able to support group projects? Are they the type of individuals that you can trust to stay away from drugs and irresponsible drinking, or are they the type that tries to drag you in to their poor decisions? Think of situations that involve a family member who gets involved in illegal activities such as gambling, drugs, or driving under the influence and the adverse effect it has on the rest of the family. The same is true for how people will perceive you if one of your close friends engages in irresponsible behaviors. If one of your best friends was arrested for being in a gang, you can imagine what people would be thinking or saying about you. Doesn't seem fair? It doesn't have to be fair. When you associate with people who are not responsible or dependable, there is always the risk that you will be seen as being just like them. Their behavior will reflect on you. Even if you have been a trustworthy person, if you have friends who have bad behavior, people that have confided in you in the past might become reluctant to trust you. Most people value the concept of being responsible and dependable.

Recently we witnessed a series of riots in Baltimore. It was a terrible display of violence and reckless behavior. People in their community had their businesses looted, and in some cases burnt to the ground. Many of the participants were young men and women under the age of eighteen. I don't know any of the kids involved, but the scenes of the looting and criminal activity will always leave an impression on me. When faced with the choice of being responsible or being destructive, they made the wrong decision.

Take a minute to think about the people and organizations that you associate with. If you sense that they act in a manner that you do not approve of, you should quickly disassociate yourself from them. Some questions that you might ask yourself:

- Are they dependable?
- Can I count on them to represent me in a responsible manner?
- Can I trust them?
- Do they have prejudices that you are not aware of
- Are they capable of bullying people that cannot defend themselves?

- How do they treat senior citizens?
- Do they drink irresponsibly?
- Do they do drugs?
- What type of language do they use?
- Do they respect others?

Take the time to assess each of these questions carefully. If you cannot honestly address any of the questions, you should think about the people that you associate with and reconsider your relationship with them.

The key is to keep company only with people who uplift you and whose presence calls forth your best.

—Epictetus

Each of you has a unique opportunity to develop your own internal network of confidants. In order to ensure that the right people are in your circle you have to prioritize the character traits that you are seeking in other people, and you must communicate your expectations. These are some tips that work for me:

- have a clear understanding of your expectations for others
- communicate your expectations clearly

- let people understand that you will not compromise your
- make integrity your highest priority
- be a person of principle and conviction
- make your actions, not your words, the model you will live by
- stand up for what is right not for what is popular
- be an ethical and moral person
- If you make a mistake, own it and learn from it

If you want to develop a tightly knit group of trusted individuals, follow the principles that I have laid out and live to those standards. When people see that you practice what you preach they will want to associate with you.

There are great examples of tight knit teams that live by their code. I remember watching the movie Top Gun on many occasions. It was impressive to see how a competitive group of fighter pilots in training to be Top Guns had to quickly assimilate into a well-oiled machine as their training ended and real-life engagement took over.

The Army-Navy football match is a time-honored tradition.

The same applies to our Annapolis, West Point and Air Force warriors that graduate from their academies and are thrust into action. It is impressive to watch the annual tradition of the Army-Navy Football game. No matter how miserable the weather is, these young men battle to the end and their classmates cheer them on. As proud as they are of their institutions, they have a greater cause and their rivals on the gridiron will be their teammates as they fight for our country.

What are the words that describe the values and characteristics that you can relate to when selecting your group of confidants? Are these words something that you can emulate in your life? How can these words guide you in selecting the right group of people? Can you describe the consequences if a team member fails to live up to their code? Just like our military heroes depend on their teammates, you too can succeed or fail based on the people you associate with. Do not be afraid to stand up for something-great. Take the responsibility, select your trusted teammates and go make a positive difference

Prepare for the increase in responsibility

When people realize that you are a person that is responsible and dependable, they will be very attracted to you. If they are friends, they will realize that no matter how difficult the situation is they can always count on you. If they are your teachers, they know that they can depend on you to be a role model for the class. If they are your coaches, they know that you will always be at practice, in the weight room, watching film, and you will understand the situation and what the coach and team expect of you. If they are your supervisors at work, they know you will be reliable and be on time and work hard. There is another great factor in being a person that is responsible and dependable, that is the relationship between you and your family. Let's take each of these examples and illustrate how they will result in increased responsibility.

Relationship with teachers: Teachers depend on certain students to lead and be the role models for the rest of the class. They appreciate students that actively participate in the class, work hard to get good grades, are courteous and respectful, and are always prepared. These are the students that teachers will eagerly nominate for leadership recognition because they know these students will represent them and the school in a positive manner and will do them proud. Can you list examples of recognition that teachers can provide? How about class president? What about National Honor Society? How about nominations to the Student ACES Program? Introductions to college admissions officers or job recruiters?

These are all highly sought-after programs and relationships, and your teacher can influence your selection. In college, teachers can help you gain valuable internships and special projects in the community. If you are a responsible and dependable person be prepared for increased responsibility in your school. Teachers will eagerly try to encourage you to step up and accept the responsibility.

Relationship with coaches: As a player and a coach I have a tremendous appreciation for the special bond that develops through mutual respect. Coaches can have a tremendous positive impact on an athlete. Many young adults today come from broken families and coaches can fill the void left by absent mothers and fathers. Coaches expect and demand respect, sacrifice, and great work ethic. If the athlete responds in a positive manner, coaches will eagerly look for ways to increase their responsibilities. Coaches seek those that lead by example to be the team captain and they also nominate those individuals to represent their school and their community in all-star games. This is a tremendous responsibility and your coach expects you to emulate all the behaviors he or she has taught you. Have you ever been in a situation where you and the coach established a great relationship? How was that relationship rewarded? I am aware of coaches that developed such great relationships with their players that they hired them as assistants when the students graduated from college. One of those coaches is the legendary basketball coach of the Duke Blue Devils, Mike Krzyzewski. Coach K as he is best known has hired a number of his former players and has been responsible for many others securing coaching positions throughout the National Collegiate Athletic Association. Many of Duke University's assistant basketball coaches are former players. That is a great sign of loyalty and respect.

The relationship between player and coach extend beyond creating a better player; it is about creating great men and women.

–Buck Martinez

Relationship between you and your supervisors: I have held a job since I was sixteen and have had the opportunity to work with many great people as a supervisor, a peer and as a subordinate. Regardless of the supervisor, in every workplace it was evident that responsible and dependable employees would see their responsibilities grow. Every organization lives and dies by the quality of their employees and by their leadership capability. As a dependable and trustworthy employee, you will be provided opportunities to represent the company in many venues. Take advantage of the opportunities that the organization provides you and make your company proud. Companies value trustworthy employees and you will represent the company in many venues. By being a dependable person you provide a great name for your company and your responsibilities will grow.

Relationship with your family: Your relationship with your family is the most treasured relationship you can have. As young children you learn to have a tremendous amount of dependency on your parents, and if you are an older sibling you will also have the opportunity to develop a positive relationship with your younger brothers and sisters. If you are dependable in the eyes of your parents, you will quickly gain their trust. This will lead them trusting you with greater responsibilities. It is likely that your parents will let you participate in some of the family's decision making. If your parents have a family business, it is probable that they will trust you to become a key member of their team. Participating in the family business will allow you to gain very valuable knowledge and expertise. There are many opportunities if you earn the trust of your family. Parents want to be proud of their children and they want their children to succeed. By earning their trust, you will be representing your parents at many functions and you will be entrusted to be a primary influence in your brother's and sister's lives.

Treat a child as if they are already the person they are capable of becoming.

–Haim Ginott

Responsibility and dependability are very important traits and when you demonstrate that you are a person who has these traits, you will be in high demand. In every phase of life you will observe that a person of trust is the one who is given all the additional responsibilities. When I was just seventeen years old, I was hired at a sporting goods store. It was a dream job for me. The owner ran many errands and trusted me to take care of the store. After a few weeks on the job he asked if I would be comfortable closing out the register every night. That was a huge responsibility and I was honored to do so. What I didn't realize was that it provided the owner tremendous flexibility and saved him the hassle of coming back every night to close the store.

When you demonstrate that you are a dependable person, people are eager to give you additional responsibilities. Everyone needs help and everyone seeks trustworthy people to help them. By having a trusted friend, student, worker or family member it allows you the opportunity to not have to do everything yourself. If we want to grow as people and if we want to be successful, it is important to have people around us that we can trust and depend on.

A person that is dependable and responsible will become very popular in every aspect of their life.

–Buck Martinez

Your rewards will be immediate

As a person who demonstrates responsibility and dependability, you will begin to experience rewards that you were not expecting. As I mentioned earlier, the more dependable you are, the greater the responsibility you will be given. The same applies to earning rewards. If you are a dependable worker, your company will be eager to keep you and that usually means that they will have to pay you more. As word gets out among the different departments at your work, or even among competitors, you will be in high demand.

As a student you will earn a reputation from the teachers and from the other students. Let's assume that the reputation you earn is that you can be depended on to be responsible and to do the right thing. Teachers will be eager to reward you with greater opportunities and will be willing to recommend you for placement. If you are in high school, it is important to develop a reputation that will create opportunities for you. Teachers that trust you and believe in you will help you to secure college opportunities and potential scholarships. With the high cost of tuition today, a college scholarship is highly valuable. Some schools today have annual tuitions that range from $40,000 to over $100,000. A teacher will recommend a dependable student over a student that cannot be trusted.

In sports, the difference between a winning team and a losing team can be the character of the players. Coaches must be able to depend on their players to meet curfews, stay away from drinking and drugs, and to be a person that represents their team proudly. There are way too many examples of players that are immature and incapable of being trusted. We read about it every day. A high school or college player that cheats can cause their team to forfeit every game. How many times do we hear about irresponsible behavior in high school, college and professional sports? A few years ago, we learned of a high school football team in New Jersey that was conducting horrific acts against their own freshman players. As part of a hazing ritual, freshmen players were being raped. The school decided to cancel the entire football season. These terrible acts are alarming, yet it seems that every day we hear of irresponsible acts that disappoint us and it some cases really upset us.

Can you think of the most irresponsible acts by people in high level positions or people in positions of trust? I can name a few that made headlines.

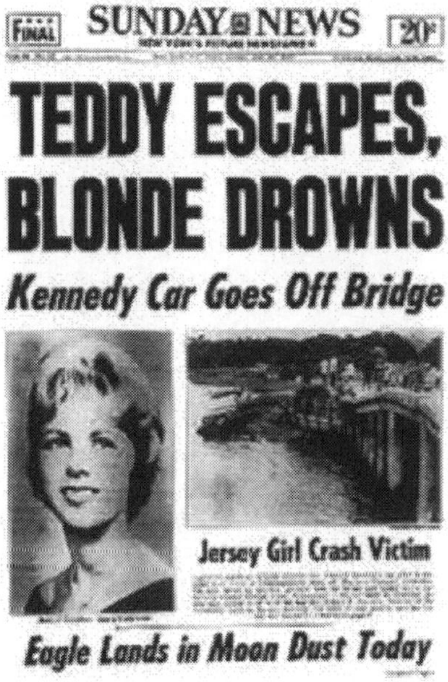
FINAL SUNDAY NEWS 20¢

TEDDY ESCAPES, BLONDE DROWNS

Kennedy Car Goes Off Bridge

Jersey Girl Crash Victim

Eagle Lands in Moon Dust Today

Senator Ted Kennedy flees the scene of an accident in which he was driving and the female passenger died: In this case, a United States Senator was driving a vehicle and crashed late at night with a female passenger. Instead of trying to help her, he fled the scene of the accident, and the passenger perished at the scene. We will never know the exact details of the incident, but we will always question why he failed to notify authorities of the accident until the next day. Imagine this irresponsible act by an individual who people elected into office to defend the United States of America. Amazingly for Mr. Kennedy, he was re-elected to the same office for many years thereafter.

United States Little League team disqualified after winning the Little League World Series: The dominant pitcher on the U.S. Little League championship team was found to have a fake birth certificate. The U.S. team dominated the other American teams and then went on to eliminate the international teams. This incident was shameful and embarrassing. After celebrating their victory and being crowned champs with media events and parades, the team was forced to forfeit its victory. It was not only embarrassing for the team, the parents, and their community, but also for all Americans.

New England Patriots Owner and Prostitution Ring: The owner of the New England Patriots was arrested in a prostitution ring in Florida. Apparently, he was at the prostitution house the day before the Patriots playoff game victory. While I find his behavior disappointing, we later found out that the girls working at the house were held in a sex slave trafficking ring. I do not think that the owner was aware of the situation, but as a high profile businessman and community leader of the most successful sports franchise in the last two decades, he should have had better judgment about his actions and how they will be viewed by the fans, the players and the coaching staff.

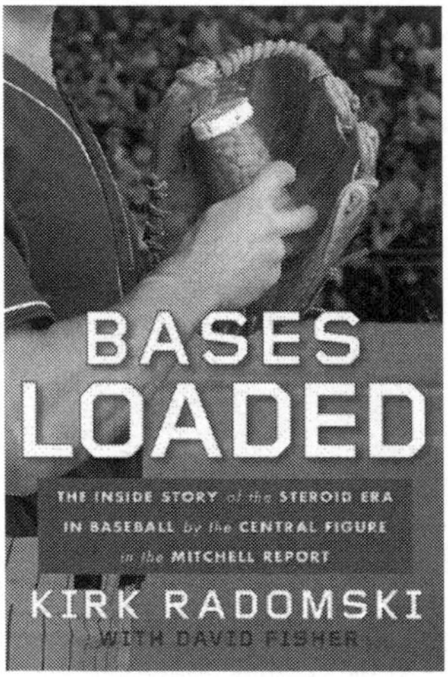

The Baseball Steroid Era: The steroid era in baseball refers to a period of time when professional baseball players began using performance enhancing drugs rampantly. Although steroid testing did not go into effect until 2003, it was obvious that players physiques were changing and offensive records, such as home runs, were being shattered. The game that had been known affectionately as "America's Pastime," was dominated by scandals, cheating and investigations. Many players were suspended during this time.

Lance Armstrong is stripped of his Olympic Gold Medals: Lance Armstrong is one of the greatest Olympians ever to have competed in the games. Armstrong was dominant in the Tour de France where he shattered records. Despite years of doping allegations, Armstrong repeatedly declared his innocence – and even tested multiple times as clean -- until an interview with Oprah Winfrey where he admitted having used performance enhancing drugs. Armstrong's confession placed a dark cloud over his career. He had been admired by all after having defeated cancer and having started a charitable organization dedicated to fighting cancer. Despite his remarkable career and world record feats, he will be tarnished forever for irresponsible behavior.

I wanted to cite a few individuals that were in remarkable positions of influence and were seen as responsible and dependable people, but will be referred to in history for not being trustworthy. I could write volumes of material on people who were trusted by the country and performed admirably. People like George Washington, Abraham Lincoln, our astronauts, our great military heroes, the nurses and doctors that care for us every day, our teachers and our police and firefighters deserve to be recognized and praised. Unfortunately, their greatness rarely gets them headlines as often as when one individual among them makes poor choices.

Being a person that is responsible and dependable takes years of doing the right thing. If you emulate the right behaviors, you will earn the reputation of being trustworthy, and that is a great thing. Be a person that focuses on doing the right thing and earns the respect of all that you come into contact with. Our country needs dependable and responsible people.

Chapter 3 – You Must Want Success More Than Others

TO ACHIEVE SUCCESS IN LIFE you will have to work hard. No matter what career you choose, no matter what school you attend and no matter what sport you choose to play, you will quickly learn that success comes with a price. You may hear an insinuation about someone that they became rich without having to work very hard, and in some cases that may be true. Maybe that person's parents were very wealthy and provided an easy path for their children. I have worked for many years, played sports all through college, and was able to get a Master's degree, and I can assure you that to be successful you have to work extremely hard and you have to want that success more than others do.

Somewhere along the road, society began telling us to take the easy way out, to take shortcuts, and to let others pay for our commitments. Maybe it is coincidence, but the federal government's deficit – the amount borrowed to finance government expenses -- is now approximately $22 trillion. The amount of personal debt affecting our young adults is staggering and there is no immediate remedy. All through life you will face intense competition in school, in the workplace and in sports, art, or any other form of entertainment that you choose to pursue. We constantly hear about the tremendous amounts of money entertainers, athletes and corporate CEOs are paid. Unfortunately, this group represents less than one percent of our population. For every millionaire, there are millions who work countless hours to get ahead – or just break even. In the entertainment world there are thousands of hopeful individuals who move to California every year to chase the dream of being discovered by a talent hunter for television or for movies. Very few achieve their dreams, while others spend years waiting tables and working long hours to make a living. The competition is intense, and the odds are against your being discovered. I applaud the people who follow their dreams and encourage those who are thinking about it. If your goal is to be the best or one of the best in your field, be prepared to work countless hours and do not get discouraged. It is important to develop a strong work ethic at a very early stage. This will help develop a solid foundation that will get you through life and you will pass it on to your children in the future.

Nobody Is Going to Give it to You

Be prepared to work harder than others if you want to achieve success. If anyone is telling you something different, you need to disassociate from them quickly. By telling you something contrary to reality, that person is doing a disservice to you. Those of you that are in high school understand the demands that colleges are placing on entrance exams and on earning top grades. The competition is very difficult, and the requirements include extra-curricular activities, such as community service. International students now take many of the college slots and they will likely go back to their country of origin with all the knowledge they gain. Not that long ago, GPAs of 4.0 were considered the best of the best. Today, we see GPAs of 4.5 and higher. The competition is intense and will continue to increase. Not everyone has the intellectual capacity to be the smartest person, but everyone has the ability to work hard and give it their best shot. Only you know when you have done your absolute best work. If you have, then you should be pleased with your efforts. If you haven't, do not go around blaming others or blaming "the system." Take responsibility for not going the extra mile and try again.

Too many people have a perception that to "make it," someone has to give success to you. That is just the wrong perception and the wrong attitude. It is good to get help. We all need help at some point in our life. If your parents can help with your schooling, you should not be apologetic for taking that help. You should be proud of yourself and remember your parent's sacrifice in the future when your children are preparing for their college years. Getting help versus having someone give you something for free are two totally different things. Getting help typically means that someone recognizes your efforts and is willing to help you by investing in you. Earning this kind of support is the product of your hard work. Getting help for college can come in various forms. If you have outstanding grades you can apply for a scholarship from the university, or from other grants that are made available. You can also apply for loans to help you meet the financial requirements. Unlike scholarships, loans typically come with a hefty price tag. You can also secure support from parents or relatives that believe in you and understand that you will put the investment to good use.

Once you get into college you will quickly find out that you are on your own. There are support mechanisms, such as tutors, available for a price. Your faculty will not be passing you along just for showing up; you have to earn your spot to progress to the next year. If you go away to school you will quickly realize that if you do not put in the effort, you will likely get poor grades. When you are paying extremely high tuition, it is imperative that you get your money's worth. Why would anyone pay to be in college and then not take advantage of the incredible opportunity to work with professors who are willing to share their knowledge? Use your time wisely, meet with your professors during office hours just to talk to them; take advantage of free programs such as lectures and events – everything you learn and everyone you meet expands your world and gives you more opportunities to make connections in your career.

This expectation that you will do your best is even more true in the work force, there is little tolerance for employees who do not put in the effort. The expectation is that you work hard for the money that you are paid; and if you do not, you will likely be out of work. Fellow employees have their own issues, commitments, and hardships. They do not have time to be watching over you. If you want to be the best, it is a good idea to discuss with your supervisor what you need to do to reach that goal. Once the supervisor sets the expectation, it would be a good idea to call a meeting to discuss and ensure that you are both in full understanding of the expectations. Once you have a good understanding of the expectations, go make a difference.

Many of the extremely wealthy and successful people in our history experienced failure and rejection on many occasions. People like Thomas Edison, Ben Franklin, Walt Disney and Michael Jordan were all rejected at some time in their life. Jordan was cut from his high school basketball team and went on to become one of the greatest players of all time. Disney was ridiculed and was unable to secure financing for Disney World. He was told that Orlando was mere swampland and no one would go to a swamp full of mosquitoes to visit a theme park. Edison failed on over 1,000 inventions before he created the light bulb, and Franklin, who dropped out of school at ten years of age, was ridiculed for many of his ideas and ultimately became known as one of the brilliant minds of his time.

The following are stories of amazing people that overcame adversity to achieve greatness in their life. They did not wait for someone else to give them a break because they felt sorry for them; they battled through their disabilities to become real life examples for others.

Melissa Stockwell: an inspiration to all

Melissa Stockwell served in the Iraq War as a first lieutenant. She lost one of her legs as the result of a roadside bomb in Baghdad, the first female soldier to lose a limb in the Iraq War. As a result, she is a recipient of both the Bronze Star and the Purple Heart. In a situation where many would have given up on life, Stockwell used her experience as an opportunity to inspire other people. She currently works with other amputees, helping them deal with any trauma they've experienced. She served on the Board of the Wounded Warriors Project® until 2014.

Stockwell was the first Iraq veteran to join the Paralympics, competing in a number of swimming events. With her prosthetic leg, she is capable of running and biking, and has gone on to become a two-time Paratriathlon World Champion.

Melissa has an incredible love of life and is known for her inspiring attitude. She has a deep and abiding love for her country and since she was a small child she has decorated her room with American flags.

Michael J. Fox

Michael J. Fox is the actor behind some of the most iconic roles in entertainment. He played Alex Keaton on the hit television series "Family Ties," and Marty McFly in one of the most popular film trilogies of all time, "Back to the Future."

In 1991, Fox was diagnosed with Parkinson's disease, a degenerative disorder that affects the central nervous system. Once the symptoms became more obvious, Fox let the public in on his condition. Since then, he has become one of the biggest voices advocating for finding a cure for the disease. While he quit acting full time, he has still managed to pop up in a number of memorable guest spots on hit TV shows like "Curb Your Enthusiasm" and most recently, "Designated Survivor." My mother battled Parkinson's for many years before it took her life. It is a brutal and debilitating disease that progressively takes away your physical capabilities. Mr. Fox has been an inspiration for many who suffer from this disease. His leadership in the battle against Parkinson's has informed and educated many people about the effects of the disease.

Stevie Wonder

It doesn't matter what age you are, everyone knows Stevie Wonder. He's the musician behind some of the most recognizable songs of all time, including "Superstition," "I Wish" and "Sir Duke." Wonder was born about six weeks prematurely which led to the retinas of his eyes detaching, resulting in blindness. Wonder discovered his love for music at an early age and started playing all sorts of instruments such as the piano, drums, harmonica and bass.

By 11 years old, Wonder was signed by Motown and had his first No. 1 hit at the age of thirteen. He has gone on to record an endless library of songs, more than 30 of which have been top-10 hits in the United States. Wonder is also the recipient of 22 Grammy awards and has permanently solidified his place as one of the greatest musicians of all time. Stevie Wonder has always had an amazing and infectious smile. His love for life has been an inspiration to many in the music profession, and to all that hear his music. He never let his disability get in his in his way and he never allowed hardship to be an impediment to his life.

In July 2019, Stevie has publicly announced that he is preparing for a kidney transplant. Now 70 years old, he is incredibly fortunate to have found a compatible kidney donor in order to have this lifesaving surgery. Stevie has touched many people throughout the world and continues to be extremely popular.

These three amazing individuals could have easily sunk into depression and despair. Each of them suffered serious adversity but refused to allow their disability to slow them down. They have determinedly continued their lives and have had a positive impact on the lives of others.

Just like the examples above, no one is going to simply give you success in life. You have to dig, you have to fight, and you have to want it. I assure you that if you do not want it, someone else will gladly take it. Be proud of who you are and stand up for what you believe in. Every day make a conscious decision to go after your dreams and do not let anyone or anything stop you. When adversity gets in your way, work around it or work through it, but do not sit idle. When you are determined, people will help you achieve your goals, but if you sit back waiting for others to get it for you, you will be waiting a long time.

Someone is eager to beat you

Do you ever feel that someone is looking over your shoulder? Do you think that someone is trying to move ahead of you at school, at work or in sports? The reason you feel this way is because it is probably true. In school, there is a ranking system that dictates what your class rank will be. The higher the rank, the better your chance of getting into a good school.

Most high school students fight hard every day to perform their best. They have to secure a great GPA and they have to constantly take tests to determine their aptitude and demonstrate that they are worthy of admission to their preferred college. The criteria used by colleges is getting harder every year and high school students must demonstrate that they have the talent to perform at the highest levels.

The number of talented high school seniors applying to college in the United States has continued to rise each year for decades. Over the next few years, the total number of high school graduates is projected to rise by 10 percent, as is the subsequent number of students applying to college — and that means thousands more applicants competing against you in the college admissions process. An additional important factor is the number of foreign students that are being accepted into U.S. universities. In some schools, the ratio of acceptance between U.S. students and foreign students is approximately fifty percent each. So, as a student, you must compete against students from all over the country and against students from around the world. Someone is eager to take your place and you must be prepared to compete at a high level.

Getting accepted into the college of your choice is just the beginning of your competition. Once you are in, you will face intense competition from other students in your major. You are all competing for the best grades, the best internships, and ultimately the best ranking. Ranking and final GPA is important for securing a job when you graduate. As a college student, it is important to be well-rounded but you must understand that you are in a competitive arena. Those that ultimately do the best work will get the best opportunities. Be prepared to compete, accept the challenges, and enjoy the ride.

Expect to face intense competition in high school and college – many others also want to achieve success, so the pressure is on!

College is an exciting phase in your life. When you arrive in college you are full of exciting thoughts. You are wondering what career you will choose, what new friends you will meet and what new interests you will develop. It is a time to engage as many people as you can and to explore all the great things that college can offer.

Academically, you should be limitless in your creativity. Try to become familiar with all the potential avenues available to you. College offers unique opportunities to study subjects that you did not know even existed, and to participate in activities with new friends.

One of the exciting opportunities that college offers is the adventure of studying abroad. One of my daughters capitalized on this opportunity and had a very enjoyable and cultural experience. College is also a time to mature and understand that you need to start developing your own ideas and to stand up for your values. You will quickly realize that there are too many people that look at college as an opportunity to be away from home and to be irresponsible. College is not cheap. It costs a tremendous amount of money and you should spend your time wisely. Hopefully, during some phase of your college career, you will develop a liking and a passion for a career or a cause. When this happens, it will encourage you to become more involved and to pursue your studies in that field.

One of the challenges of college, especially if you play sports, is the need to stay balanced. School commitments, sports, and extra-curricular activities are difficult to manage. You must stay focused on the important things and not let yourself be distracted by negative influences. Surround yourself with students that are mature and disciplined, not individuals that are trying to keep you from the things that are important.

College is competitive. Businesses are looking for students that achieve high grades and demonstrate responsible behavior. Always remember that you are competing with students from all over the world. By staying focused and by selecting a major that you are passionate about will help you stay the course and will drive your success.

The same applies in sports. If you play sports, you realize that someone is always looking to beat you out. This is evident from Little League to professional sports. There isn't a day that goes by when you don't have to fight and face tough competition to hold on to your position. Coaches also look for opportunities to create competition because they feel it will drive the players' skills to a higher level. Competition is a part of life and you should be prepared and eager to accept it. Ultimately the person that works harder and performs better will ultimately win the job. This is a fundamental aspect of life and is what will make you great. You should recognize that you will face competition and you should be elevating your game every day. When I was playing college baseball, the team would conduct an intense tryout period every year to ensure that the best players would ultimately be the ones to play. I understood that and it would bring out the best in me. Sports is all about competition and the fans eagerly anticipate the battle in every preseason to see who will get to play for their favorite team.

It is Easier to Get Ahead Than to Stay Ahead

There is an old adage that says, "the worst thing that can happen to a boxer is to win the championship." The intent of this phrase is for us to understand that when you want to get to the top, you have a burning passion and desire and nothing gets in the way of your goal. You work harder than anyone, you train harder, you eat right and you are laser focused on accomplishing your feat. When you reach the pinnacle of your sport or your goal, it is more difficult to retain the drive and ambition. People are congratulating you, everyone is demanding more of your time, and you become distracted. If you get caught up in the platitudes, you run the risk of becoming complacent. We must never lose sight of our ultimate goals and desires. Life is about always wanting to improve and continue driving for excellence. There is always room for improvement. It is easy to become complacent, so you have to always be sensitive to it. Staying on top is not easy. It requires a deeper commitment than getting to the top.

Regardless of your phase in life, sports, academics, or work, it is important to strive to grow and to get better. We can always make improvements. Life is about learning. There is an abundant amount of information available to us; especially with the internet. If your focus is to be the best at your profession, you should spend time studying and requesting time with successful leaders in your community. Listen carefully and pay close attention to what they tell you. Experience is the most valuable tool you can use. Do not be afraid to ask people to spend time with you and ask as much of them as they are willing to give you. In most cases, people are eager to spend time helping to share their knowledge. Life experiences are invaluable. The more information you can gather and absorb, the greater the amount of wisdom you will gain.

If your goal is to be the best at your sport, you must be willing to understand and to accept that you must dedicate countless hours to physical, mental and emotional preparation. You have reached the top, you understand the amount of sacrifice, hard work, dedication and perseverance that it takes. Once you are at the top of your sport you understand that you have become a target. Everyone wants what you have, and you must decide if you want to give it up or fight to keep it. You are the only one that can answer the tough question. Can you think of any college teams that repeated as national champions in any sport? The same applies in professional sports. It is very difficult to accomplish. Those individuals that have succeeded or the teams that have accomplished these goals must have amazing chemistry. Everyone has to pull in the same direction. They have to respect and trust their teammates, coaches and trainers. They also have to be willing to work harder than all others.

The Importance of Your Family

The most important aspect of your life has to be your family. Family is very different than sports or your work. It is difficult to proclaim that you or your family is at the top, but it is easy to feel that way sometimes. Imagine that your job is going great, you have a wonderful marriage and young kids. Everyone is always congratulating you on your family. It is easy to be proud, but it is also a risk to become forgetful of the things you did to develop the relationships in your family. To have a great family you have to develop great habits. It is important to spend time together, to assist your children with their schoolwork, to attend your children's events and to enjoy each other's company. Can you think of ways that would jeopardize the wonderful family situation? The following are some warning signs:

- You start to work late hours routinely
- You miss some of your children's events
- You stop complimenting your spouse
- Your priorities begin to shift towards work and away from everything else

- You allow your children's grades to slip without addressing it
- You do not take notice of who your children are hanging out with
- You fail to make time to spend time with your spouse
- You stop working out or eating right

These are some of the most obvious signs that you are not placing the proper emphasis on your family. If you allow these things to continue to occur, you risk losing your family. There is nothing more precious than your family and you must do everything you can to keep them as your top priority.

The following are some tips to helping you stay on top:

Do not let your head get too big – always remember that humility is a great attribute. Learn to be humble and understand that life can give, and life can take away. To get to the top you did a lot of things right, but you also had some luck on your side. There are many things that can come between you and being the best: illness, injuries, family issues. Understand that having made it to the top was a gift from God. Be grateful and dedicated.

Remember your work ethic -- Constantly remind yourself of the tremendous effort and work ethic that drove you to be the best Try to remember the long workouts or the long hours preparing for the big test, the big game or your big meeting. A little voice will try to constantly tell you that it is okay to take days off and to slack in your eating habits. While you are slacking your competitor will be working harder and focusing on beating you.

Develop a mental image of your goal – It's you versus your competitors. Keep a mental image registered in your mind that reminds you of your goal. Sometimes it is helpful to have a visual reminder of what you are trying to accomplish. If it is an athletic competition, place a photo of the opposing person or team in a place you can see every day. If it is a sales goal, draw a graph of your target and make it a point to check it every day to see your progress. If you are striving to get an A in school, visualize it and post it on your mirror.

You want to bring me down?

I dare you to try!

Surround yourself with the right people – You need people around you who will push you harder than ever before and will not coddle you. Too many times it is tempting to surround ourselves with people that tell us what we want to hear. While it may feel good, it is not helping you. You need people that are not afraid to get in your face and give you a dose of reality. Sometimes the truth hurts, but it will hurt much more when you fail to stay on top.

Develop metrics that track your progress against where you were when you made it to the top. It is important to understand how you are performing. Make sure you develop a series of metrics that clearly define progress against goals. This will help keep you focused on the right things and keep you from becoming distracted.

Develop contingency plans in the event you need to change your strategies. Sometimes what worked for us the first time around doesn't work the following times. Things change and we have to be prepared to adapt. In sports, there are teams that beat their opponent soundly the first time they play during the season and lose badly during their second meeting. People and teams will always be strategizing ways to defeat you, and you must be prepared to react accordingly. Do not let your guard down. Always anticipate a number of strategies will be tried by your competitor and be prepared to counter them. This happens in business all the time. New product innovation, creative branding and advertising, and customer segmentation are always being discussed in the board rooms. You must stay sharp and stay head of your competition.

You Must Stay Hungry

I have a tremendous amount of respect and admiration for individuals that perform at a high level, year in and year out. It takes a tremendous amount of self-discipline and willpower to maintain peak performance. In sports, we have witnessed LeBron James and his sheer domination of professional basketball. In football, Tom Brady and his coach, Bill Belichick have been outstanding, consistently appearing in the post-season year in and year out. In college football, Alabama and Clemson have been sharing the top of the mountain.

Serena Williams always stays hungry.

I am a strong proponent that the most dominant athlete of our time is Serena Williams, she epitomizes the term, "stay hungry." She is a tremendous competitor and gives everything she has in every match. Serena has fought through numerous injuries to remain at the top of her sport. She always seems laser focused, self-disciplined and ready for battle. She refuses to give up the top spot. I am sure that there are other outstanding athletes that perform admirably, and I do want to disrespect anyone by not mentioning their names.

In the world of business there is a tremendous amount of competition. You have to overcome many obstacles to stay on top. The competition for better and more innovative products is nonstop. It seems that everyone is tugging at your clients and the world of marketing and advertising requires daily attention. It is critical for companies to constantly infuse new talent into the organization.

NextEra Energy, A Reputation of Excellence

You have to encourage creative thinking and innovative ways to market and sell your product. CEOs have a tremendous amount of pressure from Wall Street and the shareholders. If either loses confidence in the management team, it will impact the stock price. Companies need to stay hungry to survive. If they lose their focus they will go the way of the dinosaurs. It seems that every year we see new stores emerge and we also see many stores disappear. With the advent of online sales, the retail sector has to be highly competitive. It is difficult to stay on top.

One company that not only has a great reputation but also unprecedented performance in the energy sector is NextEra Energy. They have a tremendous management team and a relentless pursuit of excellence.

Another area that is extremely competitive is television. Every year there are numerous new shows. Many of the new shows are cancelled fairly quickly while others make it. To stay on top requires tremendous creativity. You have to appeal to the audience, and you must always come up with new material to keep the fans entertained. In the world of entertainment, it is easy to be on top one day and be in the cellar the next. Your writers, producers and cast have to stay hungry and desire to be the best.

So what must you do to stay hungry and competitive? The following are some tips to consider:

Keep yourself mentally challenged – to stay on top you must constantly challenge yourself mentally. This requires focus and self-discipline. It also requires visualization, that is, the ability to envision yourself rising above your limitations. Sometimes our ability to improve requires us to be able to mentally see ourselves performing the feat. Whether it is an athletic competition, a big sales meeting, or a critical test, try to envision yourself in the moment and performing admirably. This mental exercise will keep you challenged and will help you excel.

Stay physically tough – being the best requires that you remain in great physical shape. Being in great physical shape allows you to be alert, rested, and to have the endurance to overcome any challenge or adversity that comes your way. NASCAR drivers, even though they sit for hours in a car, have recognized the importance of being in physical shape. They understand that being in shape allows them to stay alert, have better reaction time, and to have greater awareness.

Stay emotionally strong and stable – emotions play a critical role in how we perform. If you allow yourself to be too emotionally high or low, it can have an adverse effect on how you perform. Life is full of emotional challenges and they usually surface when we least expect it. There are illnesses, deaths, accidents and strains or break-ups in relationships. If you are able to keep your emotions in check, you will have a better chance of staying on top. Emotions can hinder your ability to think straight and to stay focused. It is not easy to keep your emotions in check, but it is necessary for success.

Develop and sustain spiritual strength – spirituality has a significant role in the make-up of a successful person. It allows you to stay humble and grounded. Spiritual strength also enables you to develop a faith that is very important in how you assess your vision. It also ensures that you have a higher cause in your life than just material well-being. A deep spiritual faith enables you to develop a relationship with God that will help guide you in your efforts. Having faith keeps you going in the right direction and allows you to keep the right perspective on things.

There are no accidental champions!

Chapter 4 – Establish a Positive Image

WE ALL WANT TO HAVE A POSITIVE IMAGE. We want people to view us in a positive light. What we want versus what is reality can only be determined by our actions. Our actions will define us and will determine how the world will view us. Too many people talk a good game, but their actions do not match up. How many politicians that you know talk out of both sides of their mouth? They pontificate on climate change and they live a life that is contrary to their words. They preach about moral issues and human rights, but they accept millions of dollars from countries that commit horrific acts of human atrocities.

Having a positive image requires a consistent pattern of doing the right thing. It also requires being a person of principle and self-discipline. A positive image generates tremendous value. You will be in demand and people will place their trust in you. Do you know people with a positive image? How was the positive image created? How do they sustain it? What actions ensure that the positive image stays intact? You and only you have control of your actions. You cannot control how people perceive you or what they say about you. If you conduct yourself in a manner that is morally right and appropriate, people will recognize the person that you are.

Your Actions Define You

How you carry yourself will ultimately define you. Every day many other people are observing your actions. From the moment you wake up to the time you go to sleep, you have thousands of encounters with people. Some of these interactions are personal, some are by phone, and some are via social media. Each and every one has another person on the receiving end. It is likely that you interact with your family, your fellow students, people at work, your social network and total strangers you will see at groceries, restaurants, and other places where you shop. Each person you interact with will be left with an impression of you; some will be positive, some will be negative, and others will be totally benign. How you treat people and how you conduct yourself is a reflection of your attitude. Your attitude, if positive, enables you to see the best in people and in each situation. Having a positive attitude does not mean that you won't have some bad moments and maybe some bad days; that is normal. I am a big believer in treating everyone with respect. Each of us are people and deserve to be treated with respect until you do something that causes you to you lose the respect of others.

You should recognize that not all people are the same. Some people are friendly and bubbly and look forward to social interaction. Some people will go to great lengths to avoid you and there are others that are miserable and will always seek confrontation. It is important that you recognize people's traits in people and it will help you in your approach towards them. For example, there is a man at my work that is totally inconsistent. One day he will say good morning to you and the next day he will walk right past you and totally ignore you. When I first had this experience with him, it made me upset. I thought to myself, "What a jerk." I later learned after having the experience repeat itself that the individual is an introvert who walks around in deep thought. Because of this I learned not to take his strange behavior personally. Do you know people like this? How do you react to them?

Have you spent much time trying to determine how you want others to perceive you? If you have, you have probably determined that if you treat people with courtesy, friendliness and respect, in most cases they will treat you the same. If you choose to be rude, ignorant and self-centered, people will probably treat you as if you are unpleasant. It always makes me very upset when I see how people treat others according to rank. They would treat the president of the company differently than the janitor. You should treat people the same with no regard for their title or position in life.

Having a position of power does not make someone a better person. Treating people differently based on their rank is a sign of ignorance. I always wonder how many of our homeless people were victims of misfortune. Some of them may have been military heroes who suffer from Post-Traumatic Stress Disorder, a mental condition resulting from their experiences on the battlefield. I recently watched a documentary where some professional football players pretended to be homeless. They went and lived in the streets and experienced the life of a homeless person. It is an incredibly humbling experience knowing that you have to beg for food every day. I guarantee you that if these individuals could work, they would.

Treat people the way you want to be treated, and you will begin to see the world in a positive light.

—Buck Martinez

Homeless people are humans: treat people the way you want to be treated.

One predictor of how people treat others is how they treat dogs. I have always been fascinated by the perceptiveness of dogs. Dogs have an uncanny sense for people and are very adept at sorting human behaviors. Next time you are around dogs, notice how they act towards you. In West Palm Beach, Florida, there is an animal rescue shelter called Big Dog Ranch. They do an amazing job of rescuing dogs and finding new homes for them. Most recently, they have helped find new homes for hundreds of dogs that were abandoned after Hurricane Maria devastated Puerto Rico, and people who didn't even have food or water for themselves could no longer take care of them. As part of their program they do a phenomenal job of community outreach. This provides young and old the opportunity to become educated on the plight of the rescued dogs.

When you witness the relationship of dogs and humans it is easy to predict how the person will relate to other humans. There are countless stories of dogs that have performed heroic acts to protect their owners. Dogs are a symbol of unconditional love. We can learn a lot from a dog's unselfish behaviors.

You only live once, and in most cases you only have one opportunity to make an impression. Treat everyone you meet with courtesy and respect and if you are a frequent user of social media always remember that everything you post will be read by others. "You are that which you do, not that which you say."

Image Is Not a Light Switch; It Is Constant

Self-image is the internal view or perspective that we have of ourselves; in essence, the mental image that is captured in our brain. Regardless of how we look to others, self-image is the photograph of ourselves instilled in our brain. Self-image is a topic that is extremely popular and yet controversial, because if the image that we have of ourselves is distorted, it can cause serious mental, physical and emotional issues. Self-image tells us that we are fat or skinny, beautiful or ugly, tall or short, and this self-image does not always have any correlation to the truth. In addition to physical traits, our self-image addresses the abstract issues such as, are we a good person, are we selfish, do we have talent, etc. It is an extremely difficult topic and requires much attention. In its totality, self-image represents an entire collection of our traits and brings it together in a package that represents our views of ourselves. It is not easy to discern why we see ourselves the way we do.

Self-image takes years to mold and it continues changing through our entire life. There are many factors that influence our image. If someone knew you as a child and has not seen you in twenty years, their perception of you could be very distant from today's reality. In their minds they remember you from a specific point in time, and you probably have changed significantly. How people perceive you is a reflection of your last interaction with them, some experience they have had with you, or it could be based on what someone said about you. How many times do we develop a perception of an entertainer or an athlete based on what we see on television? It happens all the time. If an entertainer routinely plays the bad guy role on television, we tend to think he is a bad guy in real life. The same applies to how people view you. If they see you through the prism of work alone, that is the impression they will have. Only a few people truly have the opportunity to see us in every phase of our life, typically your family members and your closest friends. They will always have the best and most complete image of you.

We develop our self-image through years of learning and experiences. Our experiences as a child, good or bad, shape how we view ourselves. The way our parents treated us, things they said to encourage or discourage, have had a significant impact on us. The same applies to other family members, teachers and friends. Each of our life's experiences has a definite impact on us. Imagine if you had a teacher that referred to you as stupid or dumb throughout all your early years, or if your friends always called you fat. These negative experiences, while they are not true, register in your brain. All of our relationships help shape the reflection that we see in the mirror every day. How we see ourselves may be positive or negative and can affect us throughout our lives.

It is important to have a realistic view of ourselves. We have to factor all of our assets and all of our liabilities into a collage of who we are. Based on the collage, we can develop a plan to leverage our strengths and overcome our weaknesses. We must ensure that our image is not distorted. Every day you will confront yourself with questions such as, How do I look? How am I doing at school or at work? Am I a good person? Do I treat others with respect? How we internalize and answer these questions will likely be based on our previous experiences.

If you have a favorable perception of yourself, it is likely that you will focus on how you can do more and how you can help others. A negative perception will keep you focused on your weaknesses and faults. If your perception is based on a distorted view, it can be very dangerous and can require you to get help. Self-image is very important because how we think about ourselves will affect how we interact with others, how we approach others, and how we view things.

A positive self-image can be valuable in shaping how well we are received by others. It can also be important to a well-balanced approach to life. A positive self-image will also allow us to confront challenges with the confidence that we will be successful. A negative self-image will have the adverse effect and will result in a lack of confidence and an unwillingness to live life to its fullest. I have experienced people with a low self-image and they struggle every day to meet life's challenges. Sometimes the most basic tasks are difficult and seem too great to overcome. I feel terrible for those suffering from a negative self-image. If you know people like this, always try to be positive and encouraging.

There is no formula for creating a positive self-image. It is something that you must mold and develop every day, with a number of factors and influences shaping your image. Some will influence your self-image and others will shape how others view you. Here are some tips that can help you in developing a strong and positive image:

- Learn to accept yourself
- Learn to love yourself for who you are
- Do not let society dictate your feelings
- Recognize your positive attributes
- Understand your weaknesses and develop a plan to address them
- Understand that everyone is unique and has special qualities
- Recognize that it is never too late to make changes
- Do not compare yourself to others, especially celebrities
- Talk to people that you can trust
- Focus on doing the right things
- Focus on helping others
- Ignore social media as most people only posts images that are not consistent with their real-world situation

These are things that will help you. If you feel that you have developed a distorted view of yourself, you should address it immediately. Having a negative view will hurt you and keep you from aspiring to greatness. When you focus on helping others and you take the focus off yourself, you will feel and sense gratification.

To develop a positive image, you must live your life in a consistent manner. By constantly doing the right thing you will be assured that your image is positive and viewed in the best light by everyone that you come into contact with. Image cannot be delegated to others; it is yours and yours only. Your actions will determine how you are viewed.

When you think of people that have a positive image, who do you think of? Hopefully you think of people that you know that have made a positive impact on your lives. Are these your parents, your teachers, and your spiritual leaders, people that are positive influences in your life? Are there others that you can think of?

I have been very fortunate to be associated with great people in my life. My parents, my brother and my in-laws are tremendous persons of integrity. In addition, I have been married to a wonderful woman for 39 years. She has been a wonderful wife, mother and now grandmother to four beautiful children. These are the types of individuals that you should look up to.

It is unfortunate that society tries to create role models for us based on wrong behaviors. They place entertainers on a pedestal and wait for them to self-destruct. There are some amazing people that have been influential in society and have been able to maintain a positive image. They have stayed out of trouble, they have been gracious, and they have stood for values and principles and have been a positive influence on the younger generation. Let me highlight some of these persons:

Condoleezza Rice

Condoleezza Rice was born on November 14, 1954, in Birmingham, Alabama. She grew up surrounded by racism in the segregated south but went on to become the first woman and first African American to serve as provost of Stanford University. In 2001, President George W. Bush appointed Rice as national security adviser, becoming the first black woman (and second woman) to hold the post. She went on to become the first black woman to serve as U.S. Secretary of State. She was the nation's 66th Secretary of State, serving from January 2005 to 2009.

Condi, as she is affectionately known, has always been a role model for many. She has always conducted herself with class and has never lowered her standards or her expectations. She is one of the most influential females in the United States and ranks very high in presidential polls. Condi was also in consideration for the NFL

Commissioner job. She is an amazing woman and her service to her country is greatly appreciated. Despite all of her accomplishments, Condi, has remained humble, willing to serve and graceful.

Macayla Edwards

Macayla was one of the first student athletes in the Student ACES Program. Macayla is one of the most dedicated and driven student athletes I have ever had the privilege to work with. This young warrior is a phenomenon on the national championship Florida State Seminoles soccer team and a top tier Crossfit competitor. Macayla has

endured serious adversity while at Florida State, needing multiple surgeries on her knee and her ankles. Despite these difficulties, Macayla has responded with a winning attitude and has been an inspiration to all those around her. She has a champion's mentality on and off the field and is respected and admired by her teammates and opponents. Macayla exemplifies qualities and traits that will make her a champion for life. She has impeccable integrity; she leads with honor and has a work ethic that is second to none. In a world that desperately needs role models, Macayla stands tall. I am a huge fan of Macayla and am very excited for her next chapter in life. Whatever and wherever she chooses to take her talents, she will have a huge impact on everyone she interacts with.

Dr. Jennifer Sinclair Curtis

Dr. Curtis Jennifer Sinclair Curtis is the Dean of the Engineering College and Professor in the Chemical Engineering Department at the University of California, Davis. Prior to this, she held administrative roles as Department Chair of Chemical Engineering at University of Florida and Associate Dean of Engineering and Department Head of Freshman Engineering at Purdue University. Professor Curtis received a B.S. in Chemical Engineering from Purdue University (1983) and a PhD in Chemical Engineering from Princeton University (1989). She is the co-author of over 100 publications and has given over 160 invited lectures at universities, government laboratories and technical conferences. Dr. Curtis is a recipient of a Fulbright Research Scholar Award, a National Science Foundation Presidential Young Investigator Award, the American Society of Engineering Education's (ASEE) Chemical Engineering Lectureship Award, the Eminent Overseas Lectureship Award by the Institution of Engineers in Australia, the ASEE's Sharon Keillor Award for Women in Engineering, and the AIChE Fluidization Lectureship Award.

I have known Dr. Curtis for over ten years in her capacity as the Director of the Florida Energy Systems Consortium. She was a phenomenal role model to thousands of students at the University of Florida and continues to serve in that capacity at the University of California, Davis. She carries a positive attitude and a positive self-image, which is noticeable and infectious to all that come into contact with her.

Jennifer has endured tremendous hardships in her life which could have caused her to become bitter and negative. As a young university student, Jennifer married the man she intended to spend the rest of her life with. Unfortunately, her husband was stricken with a devastating cancer. Together, Jennifer and her husband battled the terrible disease for years before he succumbed. Her strong faith in God carried her through the difficult times. She has a beautiful personality, is liked by all, and carries herself with professionalism and class at all times. She is a great example of a person with a positive self-image.

World War Two Veterans

World War Two veterans are called the Greatest Generation. They battled the Germans and the Japanese during World War II and their heroic acts allowed Europe to withstand the German assault. During the war, these brave men and women sacrificed their lives for many and prevented the Nazis from taking over much of Europe. Much has written about these brave warriors, including a television series, Band of Brothers, which highlighted the efforts of Easy Company, a parachute infantry regiment (101st Airborne Division), from jump training through the end of the war. The group was recognized for its determination, for their dedication, their sacrifice and love for each other, and their willingness to see it till the end. Many of the soldiers were wounded and many others died. One of the most amazing aspects is how many of the men returned to the battlefield after they were wounded to fight with their brothers.

Recently I had the opportunity to welcome some of our World War II veterans at the Palm Beach airport as they were returning home from an Honor Flight to Washington, D.C. I was overjoyed at the opportunity and grateful for these brave men and women. I was also struck by their graciousness and humility as I looked into their eyes, shook their hands, and said thank you for your service. We owe much to these fine people and it is a shame that they are now in the final years of their heroic lives. These individuals, collectively, presented a positive image. They are patriotic, unselfish, gracious and humble. We can learn so much wisdom from them and we should applaud them for their brave and heroic service.

Your Friends Have a Huge Impact on Your Image

I am a big believer that the people you hang out and associate with will have a huge impact on your life. There is a saying that goes, "Show me your friends and I will show you your future." There is a tremendous amount of truth to that statement. You should always strive to associate with people that will make you better. In the business world it is important to recruit individuals having skills in areas where you are lacking. Doing this will make you and your organization stronger. In sports, you are always searching for players that will complement the team; always looking for ways to improve. The same approach is required for you to better yourself as a person. If you surround yourself with people that have problems with self-discipline, engage in recreational drugs or alcohol, and lack the proper work ethic and focus, they will bring you down. You want people that will bring out the best in you. You want people that will push you to become better. You want people that are dedicated to doing the right things and living by a code of honor. You want people that are admirable. Ultimately, you want people that will inspire you to be the best that you can be. If you search for these qualities in people, you will be better and you will always be growing and improving as a person.

Sometimes people look for friends that will tell them what they want to hear. While it may make you feel better, it will not make you a better person. You need people that will give you a dose of reality. If you surround yourself with people that always coddle you and keep reality away from you, there will be a painful wake-up call one day. Try to envision going to a school where, no matter if you did well or not, you were always told that you did wonderfully. It may make you feel good, but it will not make you a better or stronger person.

In sports, I would always try to train with those individuals who were driven to be the best. I wanted someone to push me to the highest levels. I looked for people that were better than me in different areas. To be better, it was important to train with people that were faster, quicker, stronger and had better endurance than me. By training with people who possessed these qualities, it would make me better. If I couldn't get better than them, I would kill myself trying.

In school you have tremendous pressure to excel. It seems that the standards are raised every day and the expectations are exceedingly more difficult. Your school years are critically important and the people that you choose to associate with have a great impact on your success. Do you associate with people that would rather hang out all day, or people that are active and driven? Have you let people know that you intend to stay focused on doing the right things and not be pressured into wrong behaviors? If you want to attract the right folks you have to be willing to let them know what your priorities are. Making the right choices will help you accomplish your goals and aspire to success; however, if you make the wrong choices it will be a difficult road and it will prevent you from becoming the person that you want to be.

Let me provide a simple analogy. If you have a goal to get in great shape for your upcoming season, who do want to train with? Do you seek out a trainer that is going to make it easy and butter you up with nice compliments, or do you seek out someone that is going to drive you to your goals and demand the best from you? The choices are simple, but people sometimes make the wrong decision. If you want to get into a great college, how do you prepare? Do you take easy classes to artificially inflate your grades or do you take the courses that will better prepare you to compete at a higher level? The only person that is capable of making the right decisions is you. Take ownership of your life, surround yourself with people that will make you better and aggressively pursue your goals.

Life is a journey with many pit stops. At each stop there are people eager and willing to help you, but we sometimes drive right by them. Take the time to plot out your journey and make sure you pay close attention to all the pit stops ahead.

–Buck Martinez

There have been numerous stories of people that lost out on great opportunities by hanging out with the wrong crowd. During the NFL Draft, we heard of young men that were expected to be drafted in the first round, but they slipped much lower because of character issues. This typically means that the team is unwilling to spend lots of money on players that do not have a strong support system, like an Aaron Hernandez. When people recognize that you have the talent to make large sums of money they will try to hang on to you -- they want to make sure that some of your money flows their way. These are the people that you have to avoid like a plague. Try to surround yourself with people that will not only make you better, but will shield you from those that have bad intentions.

I applaud the mother in Baltimore that reprimanded her young son during the Freddie Gray protests. She was obviously upset that her son was hanging out with the wrong crowd and she was concerned for his life. She was not concerned about making the popular choice; she was concerned for the well-being of her son. These young men were obviously influenced by people that were using them to do wrong. It was shameful and disgraceful to conduct acts of violence and destruction. In many cases these young men and women are seeking the attention that they are not receiving in their home. Unfortunately, entities such as gangs provide them the support that they seek. It seems that every month we hear of many deaths in the cities of Baltimore and Chicago. These unfortunate deaths are primarily young adults who are involved in gangs or choose to hang out with the wrong crowd. These deaths are all tragic and we and our society must take action to address them. Selecting positive influences and deciding to associate with the right people will help avoid senseless deaths. The death of any child is tragic and heart-wrenching. We have to make violence prevention a priority. "Enough!" should be our motto when it comes to the death of any child due to violence.

I find it unfortunate that we read mostly about people that ended up hurt or dead because they chose to hang out with the wrong crowd. There are many examples of people that make the right choices and select worthwhile people to associate with. In every great organization there are groups of people that make a positive difference. These are the people with the right values, the right morals and the right work ethic.

Regardless of the organization that you are in, seek out good people. This includes school, sports, church or any club dedicated to a great cause. Other organizations such as ROTC and any military branch will provide great influences. One of the great organizations dedicated to making a positive impact is the Big Brothers and Big Sisters. They do great work in the community and they help identify people that will be a positive influence on a child.

We need more people to step up in this are to help offset all the irresponsible adults that have children and then abandon them.

Everyone is Watching You

It seems that everyone is watching you. There are cameras in every street corner, cameras on everyone's phone and cameras in every building we walk into. If you do something that you shouldn't, it will likely appear on the web in a Facebook or Instagram picture. There are pros and cons associated with all the technology. On the pro side, everything is instant. You can provide news and photos of an incident in a moment and you can send photos to your family members all over the world. You have to assume that everything you do will be accessible to the world and if you do not want people to see it, then do not do it! I look back to when I was a young adult and I wonder how many dumb things I did that could have come back to haunt me. Fortunately, there weren't any phone cameras or drones or multi-dimensional cameras everywhere. I guess sometimes it is better to be lucky than good.

Developing and maintaining a positive image requires that you are deliberate and thoughtful in everything you do and in everything you say. One inconsiderate act viewed by others or captured online will unfortunately determine how you are seen in the eyes of those that do not know you. Remember that your image is based on how people see you and how they interpret your actions. Many careers and reputations have been ruined by a careless act or a careless comment. Social media is unforgiving and once your actions are out in public they can't be taken back.

The best advice I can give you is to always be in control of your body. This will ensure that everything you say or do happens when you are totally aware of your actions. The easiest way to lose control is through alcohol and drugs. If you are drinking or under the influence of drugs, you will begin to lose your ability to discern what is taking place around you. Being cognizant of your surroundings is critical for your positive self-image. When you begin to lose control, you will likely engage in words or actions that are unintentional. This could affect your school records, your job and it could tarnish your family and most importantly, your reputation. Irresponsible drinking and use of drugs is not worth the consequences, or the negative impact on your health, and you should avoid it. There are way too many instances where people acted irresponsibly and were not aware of what they had said or done. Try to envision your actions as if they were being shown on the local news. That should be your barometer for measuring whether or not to do something. Can you think of friends or people that you know that were negatively impacted by something they did that was posted on social media? How did it affect them? The likelihood is that it caused tremendous embarrassment and might have resulted in the loss of opportunities at school or in the workplace.

I have spoken to many college administrators regarding the use of social media. Each of them have made it very clear that all applicants are screened and the school conducts a rigorous review of the applicant's social media to determine if there is anything that would be viewed as unacceptable to the school. Before you decide to post any inappropriate or disparaging material on Facebook or Instagram, or if you are tempted to send emails or tweets that are inappropriate, be prepared to be refused admittance to your school of choice. Schools take this issue seriously and will not jeopardize their reputation by bringing in students that can cause embarrassment for the school.

If you are not certain whether saying something is inappropriate, this is a good time to ask a mentor whether you should speak up or shut up. There is an old saying, "If you don't have anything nice to say about someone, don't say anything at all."

The same level of scrutiny applies to the workplace. When you seek employment, be prepared to have an extensive review of your profile. Companies will not tolerate anything that could be detrimental to their image. Companies will search your background as far back as high school and will also conduct interviews with people that may have known you. The search for the best employees is competitive and intense. Don't take yourself out of the running with immature acts. Be aware and be smart of how you act; remember that everyone is watching.

Getting into the best schools and securing great jobs is extremely difficult. Give yourself the best chance to excel by being responsible and smart about your social media profile.

-Buck Martinez

REPUTATION
A reputation that took decades to build can be threatened by a single event.

If you search the internet for people that have hurt their careers with irresponsible social media, you will find numerous instances of reputations being destroyed. To no surprise, politicians dominate the list. They have used very poor judgment and a lack of discretion. Athletes and entertainers are also popular in the search. There are a number of factors that are common in lack of discretion:

- Anti-gay slurs
- Racial remarks
- Lewd photos
- Tweets that embarrass their employer
- Insensitive remarks about teachers or bosses

You must be sensitive to what you say and do. One test to ensure whether you should post something is to ask yourself "How would my mom react if she saw or read what I posted?"

Your reputation is one of the greatest assets that you have. You will spend your entire life building and enhancing your reputation. Unfortunately, your reputation can be tarnished by one irresponsible act or one misplaced word. Be cognizant and be sensitive to your actions. Do not give away everything you have worked so hard for. Build your image one day at a time. Be thoughtful about what you say, don't just blurt something out in the moment. At the end of every day, think about how you have helped improve your image. Take advantage of the opportunities to improve and grow every day. You cannot control how people view you, but you can do everything in your power to assist them in their views.

The World Needs Role Models

It is important to understand the term "role model." How would you define it? Who do you consider to be a role model? What are the traits that you associate with when you think of a role model? The term "role model" is widely misunderstood today. The tag is given to many people without a deep understanding of what a role model really is. We live in a world where the term "role model" is used to describe athletes, entertainers, politicians and people of wealth. The reality is that anyone can be a role model, and it has nothing to do with their profession, wealth, or celebrity. It is about the person, their character and their heart. A role model is a person that should be followed and their actions emulated because they live a life of integrity, compassion and generosity. Their actions are based on consistently doing the right things and being a person of honor. A role model also places the betterment of the people they associate with above their personal interests. There are traits and characteristics that you should look for in a role model:

- Do they inspire you to do the right things?

- Do they demonstrate passion for their beliefs?
- Are they committed to do the right things all the time?
- Are they a person of integrity?
- Do they command respect?
- Do they earn your trust?
- Do they have a strong work ethic?
- Are they courageous?
- Are they willing to sacrifice for others?
- Are they ethical?
- Are their values and guiding principles honorable?
- Are they energetic and motivated to achieve?
- Can they overcome adversity?

These are all questions that you need to ask yourself when you are describing a role model. Are you a role model? Do others want to follow you? If yes, why? If no, why? If you are in a role of leadership, these are the questions that people will be evaluating you on. If you are a big brother or a big sister, you have an incredible opportunity to be a role model to your younger sibling.

Sometimes we become infatuated with "the stars." We admire their fame and their status. We look up to their wealth and stardom and we sometimes emulate their behaviors. It is both shallow and dangerous to think this way about people that we do not even know. The person on the screen is just acting. They are probably a totally different person when they are not acting. So, who should you seek out as role models? In my case it was always very easy because I had a mom and a dad that truly lived a life of honor. Their actions were consistent and honorable. They lived their lives to help others in a selfless manner and never demonstrated acts of selfishness.

You have an incredible opportunity to become a person of influence in your life. The world needs role models and you are a perfect candidate. If you develop and follow the aforementioned traits, you will be a role models for others. Most people are not so shallow that they only look for role models in the areas of glamor and entertainment. People realize that there is a difference between fantasy and reality. Our country is in serious need of role models, people that can step up and become people of influence that will inspire others.

I don't want to be a supermodel.

I want to be a role model.

-Queen Latifah

Every parent should aspire to be a role model for their children. There is no excuse for not doing it. What parent would not want their children to look up to them and to develop the right values? As a father, there is nothing of greater importance than setting the right example for my children and for my grandchildren. That is my duty and that is the duty that every father should commit to when they have children of their own. There is no excuse for parents that set terrible examples for their children. Children are like sponges and they will absorb everything that parents do. Take your responsibility serious and be the role model that you need to be. There are many eyes on you and if you can set the right example for them, you will ensure that many others will follow. Parenting and being a role model is a critical responsibility and is not one that can be delegated. As young adults you should aspire to make a positive difference in other's lives. There is a tremendous need for role models, and you should not have to look beyond your mirror. You are the one that can do it and the world desperately needs you. Do not look the other way when you are called. Step up and shout as loud as you can, "I want to be a role model." What do you have to lose?

Being a role model is the most powerful form of educating ... too often fathers neglect it because they get so caught up in making a living they forget to make a life.

—John Wooden

We live in a world that is anxious for role models that emulate the right behaviors. There are many children and young adults thirsty and eager to follow people that set the right example. Many children grow up watching their favorite sports heroes or following them on social media. Unfortunately, many of our celebrities fail to display the right behaviors and, in many cases, actually demonstrate terrible behavior. It is unfortunate but many of our celebrities never signed up to be good role models. It is something that comes with the popularity. I have personally witnessed the disappointing displays of poor sportsmanship, filthy language and disrespect being demonstrated in front of children and women in public settings from some of our celebrities. As opposed to presenting themselves with honor and class, some of these celebrities display rude and disrespectful behavior. What a shame. They have the opportunity to make a positive influence in someone's life and instead, blow it by using profanity and classless behavior.

As young adults, it is important to search for role models in the right places. Hollywood, sports and politics is typically not the place you want to start. My recommendation is to start with your family. I have been blessed with parents and grandparents that were wonderful role models. Both my parents have passed but their example and their teachings live on, they lived a life that was dedicated to helping others. They always placed the need of their children first and were always willing to sacrifice their time to help others in various capacities. My father, an electrical engineer by trade, helped tutor many aspiring engineers; many were immigrants that had come to this country to better themselves. I am pretty certain that my father never charged a penny for his services despite the long hours. My mom was eagerly as generous. She worked in an elementary school in the heart of an impoverished community. She would often stay late at school to help children that needed help with their studies. Their example was felt by many and impacted many lives, I am hopeful that in each of your families, there are great people with the right values. These are the people that you should be focusing on as role models.

Another source of role models can be your teachers. Each of us has hopefully experienced relationships with teachers that made a positive impact in our lives. If you had a teacher that cared or took an interest in your success, you should be grateful. The qualities that they demonstrated towards you helped you and might have significantly helped you overcome difficulties that you were experiencing. Teachers have a unique opportunity to help mold young people's lives. The great ones go above and beyond their job description to make a difference in a life. Do you know a teacher that made a difference in your life? How did that teacher influence you? Would you consider that teacher a role model?

Coach Bobby Bowden a role model for many

Coaches can also be great role models. Coaches spend a tremendous amount of time with their athletes. A coach that lives by a code of honor and a code of ethics can have a tremendous influence on an athlete. One of the greatest challenges facing our country is the breakup of the family. Too many children are growing up without the influence of a male role model in their lives. The great college coach, Bobby Bowden, mentioned that during his last year at Florida State, approximately seventy five percent of his players grew up without a father in their lives. Fortunately for many of these football players they were fortunate to play for a great role model in Coach Bowden. Many of his players still mention that he was a father and a coach. What a great honor.

"I was always going to church with my mom, dad and sister. I was literally raised under the godly influence both at home and in church," Bowden said. "There was no alcohol and no smoking at our house. That was the way a Bowden was supposed to live. My dad always told me to represent the Bowden name in a respectful manner."

As young adults, you should look for traits that are characteristic of a role model. The following are traits that you should look for in role models:

- **Trustworthy-** role models must be persons that are trustworthy. They have been able to earn people's trust through years of consistent behavior. They can be trusted to do the right thing and will not let you down.
- **Respected-** role models command respect. They are viewed by people in the community as persons of stature. They have

performed admirably and the people in the community recognize their accomplishments.

- **Caring and Compassionate-** role models are people that genuinely care for others. They have feelings and are willing to help others as much as they can. Sometimes caring and compassion are mistakenly viewed as a sign of weakness. I believe that compassion is a sign of strength and it demonstrates that the person cares for others and is willing to step up and actively show affection.

- **Ethical-** Role models understand that they must be ethical and understand that they must always do the right thing. Role models understand that morality has to be an integral component of their makeup.

- **Honest-** role models must be people that tell the truth. This cannot be compromised. Too many excuses and too many exceptions are made today for lack of honesty. Do not lower your standards and demand honesty from the people that you have relationships with or that represent you in any capacity.

- **Selflessness-** role models are people that are not selfish; they are willing to place others ahead of themselves. They understand the concept of servant leadership and why great leaders understand that true leadership comes from placing others interests ahead of their own.

- **Passionate and able to inspire others-** role models should be passionate about their cause and should have the charisma and personality to have others inspired. If you do not have the fire inside of you that burns for your priority cause, then it will be impossible to get others to feel it. Look forward to getting out of bed every morning with passion and determination to make the world a better place.

Chapter 5 – Learn to Overcome Adversity

ALL OF YOU WILL HAVE TO face adversity throughout your life. That is just one of life's realities. Adversity can come in different ways and sometimes it comes in waves. You may have already dealt with adversity. It can come in the form of sickness, disability, natural disaster, the loss of a loved one, or in the form of financial difficulty. Sometimes it is the compounding of more than one issue. The key to success is knowing how to deal with adversity and understanding that it is part of life. Many people try to ignore the issue and avoid taking the necessary steps to move forward. Failing to deal with adversity and avoiding reality can create greater issues. Ignoring problems does not make them go away; this actually tends to make the problems greater.

Have you ever seen pictures of the devastation caused by natural disasters such as tornados or earthquakes? Have you focused on the faces of those impacted by the crisis? You can see the pain and despair in people as they deal with the loss of their home or the loss of a loved one. It is difficult to watch, and you wish you were there to help. Amazingly, many of these people face adversity head on and immediately begin to repair their lives. They understand that remaining idle will not help them deal with their issues, and they begin taking the necessary steps to move forward. In many cases, they not only move forward but they also help others who need assistance. What are the qualities that help people deal with adversity in a productive manner? Each person has a unique makeup. It is hard to determine how each of us reacts to adversity because we are all wired differently. This chapter will provide a guide and a path for when adversity comes.

Adversity is a Fundamental Part of Life

Adversity is typically not something that you can prepare for. How you deal with it is usually a result of what you have observed from others in your life. Your parents are the predominant influences in your life. You have probably observed how your parents have dealt with sickness, the loss of a loved one, the loss of a job, the relocation of a family and other situations. Their behavior has a significant impact on your outlook and on your ability to effectively handle adversity.

I am a big believer that overcoming adversity creates greatness. When faced with difficult challenges, you are forced to dig deeper, get stronger and become better. There are many examples of people, organizations, and countries that were dealt tremendous hardships and were able to overcome their issues and achieve greatness. These are just a few examples of adversity that resulted in greatness.

Aftermath of the America Civil War – one of the greatest tragedies in American history is the Civil War. The Civil War was fought for various reasons, but the most emotional issue was slavery. Many Americans shed their blood at the hands of their fellow countrymen. There were approximately 700,000 casualties and many more that were injured.

Chaplain and soldiers gather to worship during the Civil War.

Despite the tension and animosity between the North and the South, after the war the states were able to place their differences behind them and move forward in a stronger manner. The country united and became the strongest economic and military nation in the world. Slavery was abolished and replaced with strong civil rights. The Civil War was probably the biggest tragedy in our history, but we were able to advance past it to create the greatest nation in the world. On January 1, 1863, more than two years before the end of the war, President Abraham Lincoln issued the Emancipation Proclamation. This historic declaration granted freedom to the slaves and ensured the unity of the United States of America.

The Emancipation Proclamation

By the President of the United States of America

A Proclamation.

Whereas, on the twenty-second day of September, in the year of our Lord one thousand eight hundred and sixty-two, a proclamation was issued by the President of the United States, containing, among other things, the following, to wit:

"That on the first day of January, in the year of our Lord one thousand eight hundred and sixty-three, all persons held as slaves within any State or designated part of a State, the people whereof shall then be in rebellion against the United States, shall be then, thenceforward, and forever free; and the Executive Government of the United States, including the military and naval authority thereof, will recognize and maintain the freedom of such persons, and will do no act or acts to repress such persons, or any of them, in any efforts they may make for their actual freedom.

"That the Executive will, on the first day of January aforesaid, by proclamation, designate the States and parts of States, if any, in which the people thereof, respectively, shall then be in rebellion against the United States; and the fact that any State, or the people thereof, shall on that day be, in good faith, represented in the Congress of the United States by members chosen thereto at elections wherein a majority of the qualified

voters of such State shall have participated, shall, in the absence of strong countervailing testimony, be deemed conclusive evidence that such State, and the people thereof, are not then in rebellion against the United States."

Now, therefore I, Abraham Lincoln, President of the United States, by virtue of the power in me vested as Commander-in-Chief, of the Army and Navy of the United States in time of actual armed rebellion against the authority and government of the United States, and as a fit and necessary war measure for suppressing said rebellion, do, on this first day of January, in the year of our Lord one thousand eight hundred and sixty-three, and in accordance with my purpose so to do publicly proclaimed for the full period of one hundred days, from the day first above mentioned, order and designate as the States and parts of States wherein the people thereof respectively, are this day in rebellion against the United States, the following, to wit:

Arkansas, Texas, Louisiana, (except the Parishes of St. Bernard, Plaquemines, Jefferson, St. John, St. Charles, St. James Ascension, Assumption, Terrebonne, Lafourche, St. Mary, St. Martin, and Orleans, including the City of New Orleans) Mississippi,

Alabama, Florida, Georgia, South Carolina, North Carolina, and Virginia, (except the forty-eight counties designated as West Virginia, and also the counties of Berkley, Accomac, Northampton, Elizabeth City, York, Princess Ann, and Norfolk, including the cities of Norfolk and Portsmouth[)], and which excepted parts, are for the present, left precisely as if this proclamation were not issued.

And by virtue of the power, and for the purpose aforesaid, I do order and declare that all persons held as slaves within said designated States, and parts of States, are, and henceforward shall be free; and that the Executive government of the United States, including the military and naval authorities thereof, will recognize and maintain the freedom of said persons.

And I hereby enjoin upon the people so declared to be free to abstain from all violence, unless in necessary self-defense; and I recommend to them that, in all cases when allowed, they labor faithfully for reasonable wages.

And I further declare and make known, that such persons of suitable condition, will be received into the armed service of the United States to garrison forts, positions, stations, and other places, and to man vessels of all sorts in said service.

And upon this act, sincerely believed to be an act of justice, warranted by the Constitution, upon military necessity, I invoke the considerate judgment of mankind, and the gracious favor of Almighty God.

In witness whereof, I have hereunto set my hand and caused the seal of the United States to be affixed.

Done at the City of Washington, this first day of January, in the year of our Lord one thousand eight hundred and sixty three, and of the Independence of the United States of America the eighty-seventh.

By the President: ABRAHAM LINCOLN

WILLIAM H. SEWARD, Secretary of State.

The first Freedom Flight of Cuban refugees arrives at Miami International Airport on Dec. 1, 1965.

Post-Castro Cuban Immigrants: Prior to 1959, Cuba was a wealthy and prosperous country. A young socialist revolutionary attempted a takeover of the government in 1953 and was incarcerated for two years. He trained in Mexico to attempt a second takeover, and by 1959, Fidel Castro, the revolutionary, was able to amass enough men and support to overthrow the incumbent dictator, Batista.

Quickly after the overthrow of the government, Castro asserted himself as the sole leader of Cuba. He denounced Cuba's relationships with the United States and proclaimed the island a communist state. He ordered many Cubans to be rounded up and executed, but many others were fortunate enough to flee the island. Castro nationalized foreign and domestic assets, with the government taking control of everything. He became a ruthless dictator and the island devolved into an impoverished, third world country. Over the years Castro depended on relationships with other dictators and drug cartels for his economic survival. Amazingly enough, Castro ruled for many years. His legacy is the destruction of a beautiful island with a vibrant economy, and hardworking and joyous people. He destroyed the economy, installed a communist system, and eliminated the motivation and initiative of the people. There might be others that disagree with me and try to romanticize Castro and his thug regime; but those that lived through and experienced the savage and ruthless wrath of the murdering dictator will always know the truth.

The immigrants that fled Cuba, including many of my family members, settled in Miami, Florida. Many of these immigrants were stripped of their possessions, humiliated, and threatened before they left the island. Most of the Cubans who fled were educated and hardworking people. They understood that despite their advanced college degrees and their mastery of a profession, they would have to start their lives over again from scratch in a new country. These entrepreneurial Cubans understood hard work and their resiliency and perseverance paid off. They created an economic boom in Miami and quickly established and inculcated themselves into the community. They used their adversity as a motivating force to reestablish themselves, and to provide a great life for their families.

The Cuban immigration story is one of determination, perseverance and success. Today, the sons and daughters of these great immigrants have established themselves as leaders in their community and will remain ever thankful for those that made it possible. Today, there are approximately two million Cuban Americans residing in the United States. Even though they are scattered throughout the country, over seventy percent live in Florida.

Malala stared adversity in the eye and persevered

Malala Yousafzai – On October 9th, 2012, at the age of twelve, young Malala boarded a school bus in Pakistan and headed to school. She was not just a student, but also wrote an online blog about life under Taliban rule to share with the world what was happening in that country – particularly the pressure on girls to give up pursuing their education. That morning, a group of Taliban terrorists approached the bus and asked for her by name. The gunman pointed the gun at her and fired three rounds at close range, striking Malala in the head. Malala was seriously injured and spent days in a

Pakistani hospital. Miraculously, Malala's condition improved and she was transferred to Queen Elizabeth Hospital in England. Malala was targeted by the Taliban and shot because she was a female going to school, and because she advocated for education of women and girls on her blog. The savage and ruthless terrorist group, Taliban, is against the education of women. Despite her adversity, Malala fought through the serious injuries and was able to make a full recovery. Instead of cowering from the Taliban, Malala became an active supporter of women's rights in Pakistan and for freedom from the Taliban's rule. The Deutsche Welle wrote in January 2013 that Yousafzai may have become "the most famous teenager in the world." Malala has earned numerous awards and recognition since the shooting.

In 2013 Time magazine featured Yousafzai as one of "The 100 Most Influential People in the World". She was the winner of Pakistan's first National Youth Peace Prize, and the recipient of the 2013 Sakharov Prize. In July that year, she spoke at the headquarters of the United Nations to call for worldwide access to education, and in October the Government of Canada announced its intention that its parliament confer Honorary Canadian citizenship on Yousafzai. In February 2014, she was nominated for the World Children's Prize in Sweden. In May, Yousafzai was granted an honorary doctorate by the University of King's College in Halifax. Later that year, Yousafzai was named the co-recipient of the 2014 Nobel Peace Prize for her struggle against the suppression of children and young people and for the right of all children to education. At age 17, Yousafzai is the youngest-ever Nobel Prize laureate.

Few have accomplished what Malala has after being brutally attacked. She has faced, not only the adversity of being shot and almost killed but has also endured the mental and emotional anguish of constant threats against her and her family's lives. She is an amazing example of how to address the most difficult challenges in life and turn them into a tremendous success story. Malala's story is one of courage, perseverance, conviction and determination. She is a selfless leader who has placed the cause for women ahead of her personal safety.

Winners Overcome Adversity

Navy Seal Teams train for dangerous situations

Each of us will be faced with tremendous adversity. It is impossible to predict how adversity will affect each of you, but certain irresponsible behaviors are likely to have a negative result. Some of the most obvious irresponsible behaviors include:

- Drinking and driving will likely cause a serious accident which could result in injury or death. The culpable party will likely end up in prison. The consequence of this action will have a significant impact on you and your future. It will cause you to forego great school opportunities and employment options.

- Texting and driving is similar to drinking and driving. Taking your eyes off the road, even for a nanosecond, can cause an accident and result in the loss of a life.

- Irresponsible sex can result in an unwanted pregnancy. Every child deserves to be wanted and loved. If you are not prepared for the responsibility of raising a child, then refrain from irresponsible sex.

- Failure to study will result in poor grades. Without good grades it will be difficult to land a good spot in a university or to secure a good job. Competing in school or in the workplace is very difficult. Do not make it more difficult by engaging in bad habits.

- Using drugs is foolish and illegal. Nothing positive can result from the use of drugs. Avoid using drugs and focus on initiatives that will help you be successful. Many drugs can be tainted with fentanyl, which can lethal even tiny amounts. Putting drugs in your body without knowing where they came from can result in the loss of your life. Be smart!

- Smoking and vaping can kill you. There's no nice way to say this, and there is nothing special about either e-cigarettes or marijuana that magically makes then "healthy." Smoke and vapor clog the lungs and prevent them from working, damage the heart, and can addict you to nicotine. Don't let a chemical run your life!

There are many other bad habits that will lead to predictable outcomes, but I wanted to illustrate the correlation between irresponsible behavior and adverse consequences. There is a tremendous amount of adversity that results from no fault of your own. Illness, natural disasters, accidents and other people's behaviors can have a significant impact in our lives. How you deal with adversity is a function of attitude. You can either make excuses or you can face adversity head on.

Winners accept adversity and are determined to overcome the challenge it brings. Adversity, if addressed properly, can help build character and make us more determined and more persistent. In sports, there are times when the star player is injured and the team pulls together behind the substitute player and exceeds expectations. The same happens in the business world every day. Key members of your team may be unavailable and other members step in and perform admirably. This is what creates greatness.

During the raid to capture or eliminate Osama Bin Laden raid, one of the helicopters carrying American soldiers crashed when landing at the Bin Laden compound. The soldiers went about their mission, remained focus and performed admirably. They killed the world's most notorious terrorist, destroyed the helicopter that crashed to ensure the enemy could not retrieve critical information from it, and brought every soldier back home safely. Despite incredible adversity, they persevered and delivered on their mission. It is hard to imagine the intensity and the adrenaline that was pumping through the veins of these heroic soldiers as they entered their helicopters for a 90-minute flight through dangerous mountain valleys to prevent radar tracking.

At one o'clock in the morning they landed at the three-story compound not knowing what to expect. Would the compound be mined with explosives? Would the occupants of the compound be armed? Would there be women and children in harm's way? Would the Pakistani government learn of the mission and try to intervene? These were all thoughts that must have been going through the minds of the soldiers as they landed their helicopters. In addition to all the activity that was going on, the soldiers experienced the soft crash landing of one of the helicopters. This created additional logistical issues and presented a real challenge to the 24 men on the ground. Amazingly, these United States heroes accomplished their mission in just 38 minutes. Their allotted time was 40 minutes; so mission accepted, mission executed, adversity faced, adversity overcome, and they still had two minutes to spare. This had to be an exhilarating experience for these brave SEALs and one that will make America proud for many years. How would you handle the adversity of the helicopter crash? Would you stay focused? How would you keep your teammates focused?

Dr. Bert de Vries and his wife Christine, an amazing bond

Dr. Egbert de Vries was an Ear-Nose-Throat otolaryngologist in Fort Lauderdale, Florida. He received his medical degree from Temple University School of Medicine and practiced over 32 years. I had a chance to meet Dr. de Vries and his wife, Christine, seven years ago. They were in a one-year leadership program with me and I had a chance to get to know this remarkable couple. Dr. de Vries was a gifted surgeon and became extremely successful in his craft.

Unfortunately, he was stricken with a very debilitating disease, amyotrophic lateral sclerosis (ALS), also known as Lou Gehrig's disease. Lou Gehrig was a great baseball player for the Yankees during the 1920s and '30s. He contracted the disease in the prime of his career and succumbed a few years later. The disease attacks your muscles until you cannot even tie your own shoes. Eventually, individuals with ALS lose the ability to stand or walk, use their hands and arms, or eat normally. In late stages of the disease, weakness of the respiratory muscles makes breathing difficult or impossible without a ventilator. Cognitive abilities remain mostly intact, though some individuals may experience problems with memory or decision-making, or show signs of dementia. The average life span of a person after they get Lou Gehrig's disease is two to five years.

On learning he had the disease, Dr. de Vries realized and had to accept that he could no longer function as a surgeon. Devastated by the reality of his predicament, Dr. de Vries and his wife turned to God for comfort and guidance. He realized that even though he could not function as a surgeon, he could teach and support other surgeons with his brilliance and expertise. Egbert and Christine seemed happy despite the tremendous diversity and accepted their situation. They realized that the odds of beating this vicious disease were not good. They dedicated their time to helping and supporting charities and to telling their story of their walk with God. They stared down adversity and with a winning attitude they stared death down.

Unfortunately, Dr. de Vries succumbed to this brutal disease, but he and Christine did not allow this vicious disease to rob them of their spirit and of their faith. They are role models to many and an example for all. If you want to know more about Egbert and Christine, their story is on YouTube. Today, Christine is active in her ministry and does an amazing job of carrying on with her husband's legacy.

Glenn Taylor is a dedicated professional. He competes in bodybuilding events and is a fitness aficionado. Glenn is also an unselfish man who spends countless hours helping others in the gym. I have known Glenn for almost twenty years, and I can't ever recall hearing Glenn complain or talk negatively about someone. He is a very positive person and is driven to live his life to the fullest. What makes this story even more special is that Glenn has been confined to a wheelchair since 1983. He was involved in a terrible car accident when he was a young man. Glenn is always willing to give advice on training, nutrition and other topics. He is a strong man of faith and a tremendous warrior for ethical and moral behavior. The following is a poem that Glenn wrote to capture his perspective on life.

LIFE, THE NEVERENDING PERFORMANCE

Life is a word that cannot be accurately defined.

Instead, life is an interpretation of the heart soul and mind.

For every person who lives in our world today, each person has a different perspective of life depending on the role they play.

You see, life is nothing more than a performance which has no time to audition or rehearse.

Therefore, life is a sequence of events controlled by an everlasting verse. Remember, unlike a screen play, life only has one showing. So, before you audition, know where you are going.

Winners help others overcome adversity

Capt. Daryl Elder, RN, BSN, (at center with arms crossed) with operating nurses and anesthesia providers at Camp Doha, Kuwait, in March 2003 as her unit prepared to move into Iraq.

Captain Daryl Elder, helping others overcome adversity

I am a big fan of nurses. They dedicate their lives to helping others and caring for them in their time of need. Some of the most incredible feats in our world have been performed by nurses serving in the military. I can't even begin to imagine the tragedy and despair that they are exposed to while performing their jobs. Many nurses have died on the battlefield while helping others. They sacrifice everything for others and spend countless hours with patients, not only treating them physically but being emotionally involved and compassionately encouraging their patients back to wellness.

Nurses have played pivotal roles in every war going back to the Revolutionary War. During the Civil War more than 20,000 women on both sides became nurses and had to observe brothers fighting against brothers and witness the bloodshed of American boys inflicted by their fellow countrymen. During the World Wars, America suffered hundreds of thousands of casualties and injuries, so thousands of nurses were flown to Europe to support the brave soldiers. Many suffered casualties of their own.

Twelve years ago, Daryl Elder, Registered Nurse, BSN, joined the U.S. Army unaware that in the future she would be an active duty captain called upon to leave her North Carolina home, husband Bill and two small children, Samantha and Jack. Her simulated combat training at Fort Polk, Louisiana, had taught Elder many survival skills, but she said nothing prepared her to live in a hostile, barren environment where ominous sandstorms stung her eyes, covered her in dust and threatened to bury her. Nothing prepared her for the high levels of anxiety she felt knowing that enemy AK47s were loaded, aimed, and ready to shoot and kill. Nothing prepared her for the loss she felt at missing a year of her children's lives.

Deployed on March 10, 2003, Elder's unit arrived at Camp Doha in Kuwait where their first duty was to set up a 70-bed tent hospital that had been stored in containers and transported to Kuwait by cargo ships.

"A typical support hospital has 276 beds," she said. "It was necessary to scale down our tent hospital to accommodate our need to move the unit to Iraq to support our mission."

On March 19, while Elder's unit was at Kuwait, the Iraqi War started. Elder's unit reached Camp Dogwood, located twenty miles southwest of Baghdad, on April 8. Two days later the first front line casualties arrived.

"At Camp Dogwood there were 2,100 surgeries performed," Elder said. "Our hospital was the busiest since Vietnam and on one night we did 300 surgeries. Each doctor, nurse, pharmacist, and technician did an incredible amount of work and made heroic efforts to save lives," she said. "Our goal was to give each patient a high quality of care whether we treated American soldiers, coalition forces, Iraqi citizens or Iraqi prisoners of war. When we did not have enough packed red blood cells on hand we had a whole blood drive, and we never rationed our blood. Whoever needed blood got it."

Daryl is an incredible testimony to the selfless sacrifice and dedication of military nurses. They work incredible hours tirelessly taking care of others. They have saved many lives and our nation is indebted to their service. They represent what it means to help others overcome their adversity.

First Responders: Giving everything to save others

One of the most heroic acts in American history was the valiant effort by New York City firefighters and police during and after the September 11 attack by Islamic terrorists. On a day filled with chaos, despair and tragedy, these brave individuals performed admirably. They witnessed horrific events including people jumping to their death from the burning buildings. Our firefighters were determined to rescue as many people as they could; in many instances, placing their own lives in jeopardy. Their heroic acts were watched with awe by a nation looking for answers.

When the planes struck the towers, firefighters and paramedics went to work. They quickly assessed the situation and began working their way through the building to treat and rescue as many people as possible. What nobody expected was that as the heat intensified in the building, the structural steel framework of the building would melt. The twin towers collapsed. All victims and first responders were trapped in the rubble and smoldering heat with no escape. Tragically, 2,743 people died in the building and an additional 343 firefighters and paramedics perished.

Those responders not trapped in the buildings worked tirelessly on the ground to provide relief to many that were injured. The effort continued for days after the initial attack as responders searched for signs of life among the rubble. Hopefully, many of you have seen photos from that tragic day. It is inspirational to see brave firefighters and paramedics covered in ashes as they tend to others in need. Notice the exhaustion – yet determination – in the faces of the heroes that put it all on the line that day. For those of you who have not taken the time to understand and appreciate the efforts of our heroes, I would encourage you to research the subject.

September 11 brought out the best in our country's firefighters, however, they are expected to perform at a high level every day. When they wake up in the morning, they do not know what the day has in store for them. Whether it is combatting a fire, rescuing a person in need, providing emergency assistance or helping the community, they do a fantastic job and we should be proud and grateful.

Police officers helping a city overcome adversity

Police Officers

We are living in a time of confusion when many of our values and principles are being turned upside down. The institution that seems to be under the most frequent attack is the police. Our police officers have come under attack by many leftist groups and by some media outlets. It seems that every time there is an issue with a policeman, the attacking groups try to generalize that all policemen are irresponsible or biased. This type of attack is shameful and disgraceful. We are all human and maybe there are some police officers that have not exercised good judgment, but I believe that our police departments do a phenomenal job of keeping us safe.

Millions of interactions happen between citizens and police officers every day of the year where nothing goes wrong and many lives are saved. We should be grateful for the loyal men and women who protect us despite increasing hostility by media and communities. Police officers are expected to address suspicious persons, enter into domestic violence situations, step into the middle of a gang war, and arrest murderers, rapists and drug dealers while remaining calm and collected. It is highly likely that in each of these situations the person that they are confronting has a weapon.

Police officers are the ones that we trust will protect us, protect our communities, and keep us safe. If they do not do it, who will? It is hard to understand when the anti-police movement started. Those that want to weaken our country surely would like to undermine our police. Those that want chaos and unrest also appreciate the attacks on police. Isn't it coincidental that when there is unrest and our police are asked to stand down, the criminals run wild, they loot, they steal and they commit acts of violence?

To be popular with protesters, many politicians jump in to make the police the scapegoat. Recently, we have seen this in New York and in Baltimore. The mayor of New York has aggressively gone after the police and it has backfired. The police, in a display of unity, turned their back on the mayor at a funeral procession for two police officers that were killed in cold blood. Ever since the episode with the mayor, crime has skyrocketed in New York City. If you don't trust your police, who do you expect to protect the city and its residents?

The same situation has taken place in Baltimore. The police are experiencing tension with their Mayor and with the state's Attorney General. The result has been a significant increase in crime and a deteriorating relationship between city officials and their police department.

We have to trust that our police will work hard to protect us. That is what they are supposed to do. Police officers do a tremendous job in keeping calm and peace in their neighborhoods. They help many and do a great job of protecting our children. They often step up to help people that are dealing with serious adversity. They are placed in very difficult situations, such as domestic disputes, burglaries, attempted murders and other dangers. They also take care of everyday issues such as helping a child get home safely or keeping a homeless person safe. They are heroes to many and deserve our respect and support.

Just like our firefighters, police officers performed admirably during the September 11 attacks. They worked tirelessly and sacrificed endlessly. Over seventy officers gave their lives while supporting others. The next time you hear derogatory statements about our officers, or if you hear the media attempting to drive a wedge between the community and the police officers, take the time to assess the situation and conduct your own research. I assure you that in each case you will come to the conclusion that your officers do a real good job of keeping you safe.

A local Afghani woman, from the Kuchi Tribe, located in the city of Gardez, Afghanistan, tries to comfort her daughter, as US Army Major Mary V. Krueger, 321st Civil Affair Battalion, gives the child an examination. MAJ Krueger is assigned to the Surgeon Cell for the Combined Joint Civil Military Task Force, which together operate an ambulatory clinic providing vaccinations, acute and preventive medical care for members of the local Tribes.

Soldiers help children in war-torn countries

Other than the Civil War, Pearl Harbor, and September 11, our nation has been spared the brutality of war on our soil. We are fortunate that the brave men and women in the military do an amazing job of battling overseas to protect our freedoms here at home. I have never served in the military, but I have tremendous respect, admiration and gratitude for those that have served. It is amazing to see that despite the fact that we engage in a war against an enemy, our soldiers demonstrate affection and compassion for children that to no fault of their own are caught in the situation. Many of these children have to watch the destruction of their homes and in many cases, the loss of their parents. It would be understandable for our soldiers to show animosity towards everyone they confront but instead, they perform acts of generosity and valor, sometimes placing their own lives at risk to rescue children in harm's way. What makes this situation more compelling is that our enemies have sometimes used children as bombs. They attach bombs to their bodies and have them approach our soldiers. This tactic was used in Vietnam and continues to be used in the Middle East and Africa.

Children living in war-torn countries face tremendous adversity in their lives. In many cases, they have lost their homeland, their homes have been destroyed, and they may have lost their parents; their lives have been turned upside down. Due to the compassion and generosity of our soldiers, they are removed from harm's way, they are provided food and shelter, and they are provided drinking water. Many of these children will face emotional and mental scars; yet having the support of our men in uniform will help with their struggle. It takes a special type of person to be able to put aside the differences that exist between two governments and to accept the children. Our brave men and women have been doing this throughout our nation's history.

I strongly believe that we live in the greatest country in the world. We have traditionally been the defender of those that cannot defend themselves. We have been the compassionate and generous superpower. It is appalling to see fellow Americans that burn our flags and portray our country in a negative light. Sometimes you have to travel outside the United States and see the situations people deal with daily in other parts of the world to truly appreciate the greatness that we have. I can only wish that individuals that do not like this country take the time to reflect what they have before they speak. They also have the opportunity to move to another country if they wish to. Nobody is forcing them to stay.

Winners understand servant leadership and dedicate their lives to helping others overcome adversity.

—Buck Martinez

Winners handle adversity with class

Adversity can be painful, it can be distracting and it can keep us from achieving our goals. Winners understand that adversity is difficult but they also understand that feeling sorry for yourself is not the proper course of action. Winners understand they have to get back on their feet and they have to keep moving forward. Feeling sorry for yourself or wanting someone's pity is not the way to deal with adversity. Winners face adversity with class and dignity. They do not make excuses. In many cases, people do not even know that the individual is dealing with tough issues because they have kept it to themselves. There are many individuals that have faced adversity with class and came out stronger.

Two of the most amazing incidents happened to world leaders. Both Ronald Reagan, the 40th President of the United States, and

Pope John Paul faced death when they were in office. President Reagan was shot and Pope John was stabbed. Neither of these men tried to sensationalize the issue. They quietly accepted their fate and continued their mission of serving others. They never shone attention on themselves, they focused on others. There are other individuals that also warrant respect and admiration for how they conduct themselves through their adversity.

TBS broadcasters Cal Ripken, Jr. and Ernie Johnson, Jr. – New York Yankees at Baltimore Orioles. ALDS Game 1. October 7, 2012.

Ernie Johnson Jr. is a sportscaster for Turner Sports and CBS Sports. Johnson is currently the lead television voice for Major League Baseball on TBS, hosts Inside the NBA for TNT, and contributes to the joint coverage of the NCAA Division I Men's

Basketball Tournament for Turner and CBS. Ernie enjoys a very positive reputation on the air and he is beloved by the people he works with. It seems that Ernie is working on every major sports event on television. Ernie has covered baseball, basketball, golf, The Olympics and football on television. He has become the go to guy when covering major events.

In 2003, Johnson was diagnosed with non-Hodgkin's lymphoma, but continued his work through June 2006, when he began treatment. Despite his sickness, Ernie maintained his lively and positive spirit. He did not let cancer take away his spirit. Cancer was not the only adversity that Ernie would face. With two biological children of their own, Ernie and his wife decided to adopt four additional children, two of them from different countries. One of his adopted sons is Michael; they adopted him from an orphanage in Romania, despite being aware that Michael had serious complications. He was 3 years old when Cheryl, who had seen a television report on deplorable conditions in faraway orphanages, journeyed to Bucharest in hopes of adding the first adoptee to the Johnson home.

For Cheryl, it was love at first sight when she noticed a tiny boy, who had not learned to speak, couldn't walk and had a clubfoot. Abandoned soon after birth, the boy was confined inside the orphanage building since the day he arrived. As Cheryl tried bonding with him, she took him outside. Terrified and unable to focus, he screamed in horror when exposed to the alien sunlight. Cheryl called Ernie back in Atlanta and told him she had found their new son. She told her husband everything.

"If I leave him here, I'll wonder what happened to him for the rest of my life," Cheryl said.

"It's time to bring him home," Ernie told her. A year later, in 1992, Michael was diagnosed with muscular dystrophy. In 2001, he fell and broke a hip, which ultimately sentenced him to life in a wheelchair. Michael's specific diagnosis is Duchenne Muscular Dystrophy. There is no cure. It only gets progressively worse. Doctors have told the Johnsons that statistics show that Michael, who is now 27, might not make it to his 30s.

Ernie has battled through his cancer and through his son's very difficult disease. Throughout this adversity, Ernie has remained amazingly confident. He has a tremendous love and bond for his family and has never demonstrates any anger or self-pity. He has carried himself with class and he credits his Christian faith for his strength.[1]

South Carolina Church Shooting

In one of the saddest and most tragic days in our history, nine innocent people were struck down in cold blood by the face of evil. A 20-year-old man full of anger and hate calmly walked into a church prayer group and began shooting strangers. I cannot explain why things like this happen, and I am at a loss for words over the sadness and grief for the victims and their families.

---

[1] http://www.dallasnews.com/sports/more-sports/headlines/20140328-final-four-broadcaster-ernie-johnson-embraces-wonderful-life-with-disabled-adopted-son.ece

Charleston, South Carolina came together as a community to pray and support the families of the shooting victims, who asked for peace and unity, and forgave the murderer.

Of all the places where you expect to find peace and solace, it was in a church where a person without emotion killed them. This is a devastating event because the killer claimed racism as his motive. It is incomprehensible how someone can hate because of skin color. How could this young man hate so deeply at such a young age? What could possess him to strike down people in the House of God? At a time when our country has made so much progress on the race issue, we have had a careless act of evil infused into our society.

The families of the nine victims have every right to want justice and revenge, but instead, we have seen genuine and compassionate people coming together to grieve as a community. Despite immense adversity, these family members have handled this tragic situation with dignity and class. When facing the stone-cold killer in the courtroom, they actually told him that they forgave him. These individuals have taught us so much. They could have spouted anger and called for demonstrations, but instead they asked for peace and unity. They are truly amazing people and we should be using them as examples. No one deserves to lose a loved one the way they did, but yet, they have shown tremendous courage, love and compassion.

At a time of personal loss and tragedy, true strength is required to persevere. Be a person that handles situations with dignity, class and grace.

–Buck Martinez

President George W. Bush and Wounded Veterans

Every year, former President George W. Bush invites wounded veterans to his ranch in Crawford, Texas for some mountain biking fun. The Annual Warrior 100K is a three-day bike ride to honor service members injured in Afghanistan and Iraq. President Bush invites military veterans, many of whom were seriously wounded in the wars he initiated while he was in the White House. President Bush has always had an incredible appreciation and genuine compassion for those who served our country, and for those injured in doing so. It's a ritual of thanks and bonding that might seem fraught from the outside, but everyone who takes part in the event seems to enjoy. Despite the grueling three-day event in which, participants bike through treacherous and narrow woods, everyone enjoys the challenge and the camaraderie.

Our wounded heroes have experienced serious adversity; many have lost limbs and suffered from serious depression. It is inspiring to see these brave and courageous men and women engage in this event. They have stared adversity down and have overcome adversity with class and dignity. It takes tremendous courage to be able to face the challenge of losing a limb or multiple limbs. Despite these serious setbacks, our soldiers are able to participate in events such as Bush's challenging mountain biking event. Their participation is uplifting and inspiring. It should help all of us who are dealing with our own adversity to develop the necessary strength to fight through it.

"These vets are setting an example to other citizens who might be complaining about their fate in life," Bush said.

These examples illustrate how people deal with adversity. It is difficult to gauge what is happening in people's lives. We know very little about most people, even those you meet at school, at work, or in your social life. Before you pass judgment on somebody, take time to recognize that they may be going through a difficult time in their life. Dealing with adversity is difficult; when adversity comes your way, stand strong and handle it with class.

Adversity Builds Character

We all face adversity and will continue to face it throughout our lives. How we face adversity and how we deal with it will either build character or make us weaker. It is difficult to understand how you will handle difficult issues, or how you will fight through pain and suffering. It is impossible to gauge how you will react if the dream you are pursuing is shattered. Until you are tested, you will not know. This applies in all walks of life. Try to remember the first school test that you did poorly on and you didn't know how to react. You thought you had given it all, but then you studied even harder and applied yourself more and you received an A. If you had not done poorly, you would not have known how much more you had in you.

In sports, you trained harder than you have ever trained and you still lost badly. When this happens, you have a choice: you can either settle for less, or you can train harder. Until we push ourselves beyond what we are capable of, we will not know our limits. To be successful, you have to fight through disappointments and failures. Fighting through it is what creates the tenacity to get better. Those willing to do this develop character. I am a firm believer that to be the best you have to work harder, train harder and learn to compete. When things do not go the way you expected, you have to find a way to battle through. If you are too comfortable in your current situation, you will not want to work for more. Set your goals high and be willing to accept adversity to attain them. You will recognize that battling through adversity builds character.

You may encounter many defeats, but you must not be defeated. In fact, it may be necessary to encounter the defeats so you can know who you are, what you can rise from and how you can still come out of it.

–Maya Angelou

When I was a freshman in high school, I was expected to be a star pitcher. I was very successful through Little League and had played on the high school team as an 8th grader, on their summer team. After finishing the freshman basketball season, it was time to join the baseball team. I was excited to play baseball and welcomed the challenge.

During the first week of practice, the pitchers were going through their drills when I heard a pop in my shoulder. The pain was excruciating, and I knew that there was something terribly wrong. The news from the doctor was devastating. The doctor said that the injury was a result of overuse, I would not be able to play the entire season, and that the odds of pitching again were slim to none. During this period, the 1970s, physical rehabilitation was non-existent. The standard remedy was to give you a series of cortisone shots. I later learned that cortisone actually causes tremendous damage around the area where it is injected.

Adversity hit me at an early age, and I was determined to overcome it. Baseball was my passion and my dream was to be a major league baseball player. The day after the devastating news, I began teaching myself to throw left-handed. I threw more left-handed in a short period than most people throw in a few years. I was determined and relentless to play my sophomore year as a lefty. Throwing lefty did not come naturally, but through repetitive training every day the motion became more natural. I played first base as a lefty in some winter leagues and outfield on some men's softball leagues. Later in my junior year I pitched lefty and righty in a summer league game.

Unfortunately, despite much training, my right arm was never the same. I had to sit out my junior year after re-injuring the arm before the season. I felt crushed, but not beaten. I was able to play third base during my senior year in high school and played four years of college baseball as a third baseman and as a catcher. Despite not regaining the velocity that I had, dealing with adversity taught tremendous and valuable lesson about life. These include:

- Never let someone tell you it can't be done
- When a part of your body is injured, other skills can be learned and improved
- Mental toughness is a critical component for success
- The skills that you learn in dealing with the physical challenges can be applied to other phases in life

- The desire to compete carries forward throughout your adult life
- Never quit
- If you have a dream, pursue it to its fullest
- Be willing to use your experience to help others

To this day, my greatest motivation comes from hearing words such as, "it can't be done" or "You can't do it." These are words that instill in me a fighting spirit and a relentless desire to achieve. What are the words that make you a fierce competitor?

NASA Challenger Disaster

On January 28, 1986, NASA Space Shuttle Challenger lifted off from the John F. Kennedy Space Center in Florida for flight STS-51-L. It was a much-anticipated flight as a science teacher from New Hampshire and a strong advocate of space exploration was selected to join the astronauts on the mission. Challenger launched at 11:38 a.m. Eastern Time in front of more media attention than usual, as many wanted to see the first teacher go into space. Christa McAuliffe, the schoolteacher, was planning to give lessons while in orbit.

The crew of Space Shuttle mission STS-51-L pose for their official portrait on November 15, 1985. In the back row from left to right: Ellison S. Onizuka, Sharon Christa McAuliffe, Greg Jarvis, and Judy Resnik. In the front row from left to right: Michael J. Smith, Dick Scobee, and Ron McNair.

She and the rest of the crew never made it. Challenger broke up 73 seconds after launch in front of the television cameras. "Flight controllers here are looking very carefully at the situation. Obviously, a major malfunction," the NASA launch commentator said as pieces of the shuttle fell from the sky into the Atlantic.

I vividly remember that tragic day. Many of us at work were watching in disbelief, not wanting to ask questions, fearing the answer that we did not want to hear. Shortly after takeoff, it was obvious that something was wrong. A tremendous amount of smoke was visible high in the air. NASA had always been a proud institution of the United States and it was shocking to see this tragedy take place right in front of our eyes. NASA was devastated and announced a thirty-two-month shut down to assess the failure.

NASA came back stronger than ever with determination and resilience. The Challenger disaster was serious enough to make our great nation second guess its commitment to the space program. Instead of cowering to the pressure to shut down space exploration, NASA went forward boldly. Adversity built tremendous character and made them stronger.

Ronald Reagan, United States President at the time of the Challenger disaster, said at the dedication of the memorial, "We will never forget them, nor the last time we saw them, this morning, as they prepared for their journey and waved goodbye and 'slipped the surly bonds of Earth' to 'touch the face of God.'"

Sometimes when we reach for the stars, we fall short. But we must pick ourselves up again and press on despite the pain.

–Ronald Reagan

Chapter 6 – Be Honest With Yourself

TO BE SUCCESSFUL YOU HAVE TO BE HONEST with yourself. You know yourself better than anyone else does. You know your strengths. You know your weaknesses. You understand the things that make you smile, and you understand the things that make you cry. Despite what others think and say about you, you and only you know the truth. You understand what motivates you and you recognize things that do not matter. It is important to recognize that you can only be yourself, you can't try to be somebody else. Being honest with yourself takes a tremendous amount of courage.

Sometimes the things that we aspire to are the things that we just do not have a talent for. For example, I love music, but I have the worst singing voice and I have no rhythm. I watch people dance at weddings, but my feet refuse to move in any kind of rhythm. I feel sorry for my wife because she enjoys dancing, but it is something that we have not been able to share because of my lack of talent. Each of you are special and each of you have special gifts and unique skills. Some of you might be good at math and science while others might have a gift for English and journalism. The sooner that you can be honest with yourself is the sooner that you can begin to focus on your skills.

Over the years I have coached many children. Some have been very talented in their sport; others have been mediocre, and others just have not been blessed with skill in that sport. Not surprisingly, the parents spend a tremendous amount of money on lessons to make their child better. Whether it is golf, baseball, tennis or piano, parents are determined to make their child the next superstar. In many cases, the child has no interest in the activity. It is unfortunate that so many parents fail to listen to their children. In other cases, the children are afraid to let their parents down. Always remember that your parents want the best for you and even though they might push too hard, they do it with your best interest at heart. It is important to be honest with yourself about your interests. If you do not speak up, you could be trapped in something you do not want to do.

Try to envision what you would like to be in the future. Can you envision yourself in that ideal role? Now, think about what it takes for you to learn that skills and reach that capacity. Is what you are doing now the best preparation? If not, what must you do to change course? These are the tough questions that you must be willing to ask yourself. It is your life; it is your future and it is your destiny. You must be the one that makes the decisions.

As a young adult you have many people giving you advice. It is important to listen, especially to people that you trust and respect. Assimilate the advice they provide and carefully think through what people are telling you. Assess everything they offer you with care and make an honest evaluation. You are the only one that can determine what your interests are and if this is an area that you are strong in. Be open minded but be honest with yourself.

Take a hard look in the mirror

Have you ever taken a hard look in the mirror? It should not be an intimidating place. It should be a place where you can have a genuine and honest conversation. Mirrors do not lie; they merely reflect an honest perspective. If your parents and your guidance counselors think that you should study engineering, but the mirror tells you that your interests are in business or philosophy, then you should listen to the mirror. The important perspective is honesty – be honest with yourself. If you do not want to be an engineer because it might be too much work, you have defeated yourself before you have even given it a fair shot. The key is that if your heart is in something other than engineering, you go for it. Be the best at whatever you decide to pursue. Make your decisions based on honest feedback. What are some of the tough issues that you have to be honest with yourself about? These questions might help:

- Am I trustworthy?
- Am I a hard worker?
- Do I prepare to the fullest before every exam?
- Do I command respect?
- Do I portray a positive self-image?
- Do I listen attentively?
- Am I honest?
- Am I selfish?
- Do I stand up for those that can't protect themselves?
- Do I avoid alcohol if I am under eighteen and do I act responsibly if I am over eighteen?

- Do I have a clear vision for my life?
- Am I emotionally strong and capable of handling adversity?
- Am I driven to succeed?
- Do I depend on others to carry me?
- Would I rather follow than lead?

These are questions that only you can answer. The toughest judge of honesty should always be you. You know yourself better than anyone else.

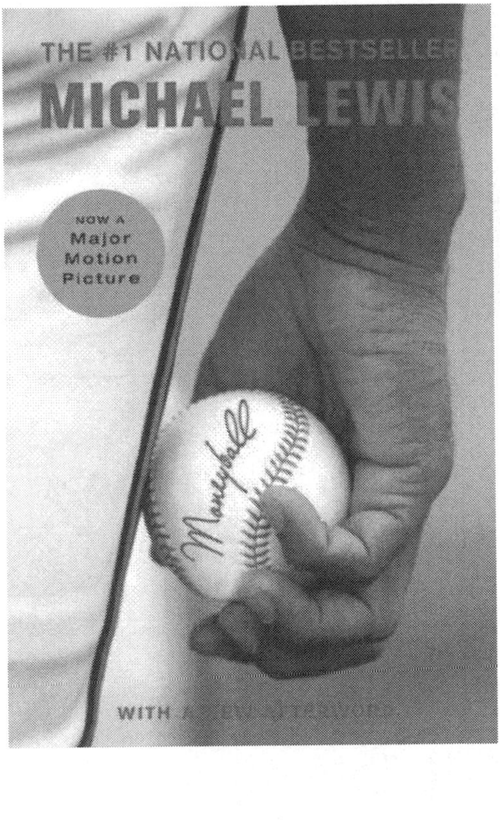

In the book *Moneyball: The Art of Winning an Unfair Game*, we learn much about the main character, General Manager Billy Beane. Beane was an amazing high school athlete, excelling in baseball and in football. Beane was so gifted that Stanford University recruited him to be the successor to legendary quarterback John Elway, and he was also drafted in the first round of the Major League Baseball draft. Imagine two different sports competing to recruit you and having the option to pick your favorite! Beane decided to forego college, where he would have received a full scholarship to one of the finest universities in America, Stanford. When reading *Moneyball*, I got the impression that Billy's first love was football. When he chose a career in baseball, I had to wonder if he was honest with himself. Though he has become a very successful baseball executive, he never experienced the opportunity to play college football in one of the greatest venues.

Be what you are. This is the first step towards becoming better than you are.

–J.C. Hare and A.W. Hare

Seek feedback

For you to continue to grow as a person it is important to seek feedback from others. Just like being honest with yourself is important, so is seeking the feedback that can help you develop. This requires that you be receptive to someone giving you input about yourself. If you do not really want it, don't ask for it because it will create an unpleasant situation. Let's assume you are making a big presentation at school and you ask your best friend to critique your presentation. After you finish, he says that it was lacking inspiration and you should consider starting from scratch. First, you should thank your friend for providing feedback. Then you should ask for specific areas that he feels could be improved, and finally you should request that he agree to review your next draft. By doing this, your friend will feel valued and eager to help you. If you became defensive about the feedback after you were the one to ask for it, the likelihood is that your friend would respond in a negative manner. For example, "Why did you ask for my feedback if you didn't really want it?" He could also get angry and say, "Why did you waste my time?" Seeking feedback requires that you have an open mind and be willing to accept critique that might be difficult. Accepting feedback doesn't mean that you have to do what someone's feedback suggests; it provides you with an additional viewpoint to consider.

When seeking feedback, it is important to be clear about what you need. You should request a few minutes with the person you will be requesting feedback from and tell them that you are interested in being successful and growing as a person. In addition, let the other person know that their input is very important to you and that you value their opinion. You can also request that they continue to provide you feedback as they interface with you through work or school or your sports team.

Feedback is critical in every walk of life. As a student it is important to hear from a teacher how you can improve in your schoolwork or how to develop more effective means of communication. Feedback from teachers is critical for student development. A good teacher should be eager to support the students and to provide them guidance and counsel in their schooling and their future. If a teacher doesn't provide feedback, then you should request some time to seek guidance and direction. Teachers have a significant influence on your life, and they can be instrumental is assisting in your development. Do not be shy or embarrassed to approach a teacher. Most teachers are eager to help and support you.

Seeking feedback is important to your development

Coaches can also be great sources of feedback. They are interested in your well-being and want to help. Coaches have tremendous insight into your development and should be a great source of information. Whereas teachers have observed you in the classroom and on projects, coaches have seen you in competitive situations. They understand how you compete. They have observed how you perform under pressure, and most importantly, they have witnessed your teamwork skills. Coaches have valuable insight and should be a source of feedback for you. Though some coaches may appear tough and uncaring, I have found that the vast majority deeply care about their players. Talk to your coaches and ask them to provide you candid feedback on areas that will make you a better person.

Ultimately, parents and other family members should be your best source of feedback. They have spent their entire life with you and have a good appreciation for your talents, your emotions and your aspirations. The greatest love in your life will always be your family; you might have differences, but a family's love is unconditional. Ask your family to provide you the necessary feedback for improvement. If your family brings something to your attention that you do not agree with, ask for examples and ask for clarification. When seeking feedback, you must have a solid understanding of what someone is telling you. Lack of clarity will not help you and can also lead to confusion.

One of the most common tools that organizations use for providing feedback to their employees and managers is a 360-Degree Feedback exercise. The exercise requires that the employee's peers, supervisor, and others that work closely with them provide honest feedback in a confidential manner – their names are not revealed so they can feel comfortable being completely honest. The exercise provides important information and is very useful for the employee's development. The exercise is only effective if the participants provide candid and honest feedback. After the feedback, the employee is expected to develop a game plan to address any issues that surfaced during the exercise. This exercise provides you with the opportunity to see how others perceive you. The exercise also requires that you take the same questionnaire that is given to those providing feedback about you; this allows you to assess areas where there is a gap between how you see yourself and how others do.

When there is a gap between how you perceive yourself and how others do, it is referred to as a blind spot. We might have a behavior we aren't even aware of that has a negative effect on people. If no one makes us aware of it, we will continue annoying people. Feedback is important in the uncovering of blind spots. Once you are made aware of your blind spot, you can feel free to discuss it openly with people and let them know that you were unaware, and you meant no harm by your behavior. Doing this can help improve relationships for you.

If you do not tell the truth about yourself you cannot tell it about other people.

–Virginia Woolf

Understand your strengths and weaknesses

Every person in the world has a unique fingerprint. When you begin to look at the this fact the complexity of human uniqueness is staggering. There are over 7.5 billion people in the world, and each of us is created differently. We all have unique talents and we all react in our own way to situations. I might get all teary-eyed and choked up when a dog is injured in a movie, and others will not have any reaction. What makes us different can also make us great. It is important to understand our strengths and weaknesses. This will help us determine what we want to study. It will help us find the right path in our employment and it will help us find the right person that we will marry one day. By understanding your make up, it will help you make better decisions in all aspects of your life.

Do you know what your strengths are? Do people give you feedback on your strengths? How do you know if your perceived strengths are real? It is not easy to understand your strengths. You might have an idea of your strengths, but you may have never been tested. When we think of strengths, we tend to think of things that are tangible. For example, are you smart, are you good at sports, are you a good dancer? These are all things that people will easily recognize, but there are more important things that are intangible and more difficult to measure. Some hidden strengths that might apply to you:

- Am I trustworthy?
- Am I dependable?
- Am I caring?
- Am I easy to talk to?
- Am I generous?
- Am I a good listener?
- Am I compassionate?
- Am I willing to stand up for my friends?
- Am I willing to improve?
- Am I willing to accept feedback?

There are also weaknesses that you want to identify to understand yourself better:

- Am I greedy?
- Am I boastful?
- Am I self-centered?

- Am I a gossiper?
- Am I arrogant?
- Am I undependable?
- Am I uncaring?

When you assess your strengths and weaknesses, these are the type of characteristics or traits that you should pay attention to. These are traits that you can address and change. You are never too old to learn, and it is never too late to transform. If you are provided with feedback and it contains some of these negative traits, make a conscience decision to change. As young adults you have your entire future ahead of you, so work to develop the traits that will help you in life.

Do you remember the story of Ebenezer Scrooge, the elderly miser, told in the Charles Dickens classic *A Christmas Carol*? Scrooge was confronted by the spirits of Christmas Past, Christmas Present and Christmas Future, who showed how his greed and withdrawal from the joy of life had shriveled him up into sadness and resentment. He decided to change from a greedy and stubborn person to a generous and compassionate one, and his life was enriched and made whole again. This happens every day in life.

Listen to those providing you feedback, look in the mirror and understand your strengths and weaknesses. Self-evaluation is a powerful exercise, but it can be the opportunity to set a successful path for the rest of your life.

Leverage your strengths

Have you ever been around a person that has tremendous talent but refuses to see it? I have been around many people trapped in careers that don't represent the best use of their talents. They come to work every day and they do a good job, but they are not happy. In many cases they are afraid to leave their comfort zone. They may have financial issues or family issues that make it difficult to leave. Everyone sees the tremendous talent that they may have beyond what they are currently doing, but something is holding them back from change. In all my years in business, I have had the opportunity to work with many great people in many different capacities. Sometimes the hidden talents that people possessed were very obvious, and I could also see that they were holding back. Unfortunately, life is very short and if you do not release your hidden talents, you will regret it in the future.

You should leverage your strengths. Each of you possess tremendous talents: be able and willing to enjoy them. Many professional athletes have successfully transitioned their careers from professional sports to the world of broadcasting or business. This requires that you understand your strengths and that you are willing to work hard to transition into your new career. As I mentioned earlier, there are physical talents and intangible talents. The most difficult transitions are those that require you to change from the person that you are now into the person you want to become. If you grew up in an environment where trust was not demonstrated, it is highly likely that you are not a trusting person. It will require many experiences with good and honest people before you can change. The same applies to people raised in an environment where they were taught to get as much as they could for themselves. For anyone who experienced this, it will be difficult for you to learn to be generous and selfless. We may not know what strengths we are capable of because we haven't been exposed to those behaviors. It takes a willingness to look beyond the boundaries of your experience and see what you can become.

When I was a young boy I would observe the ushers at church. They typically stood in the back of the church and were somewhat emotionless. What I didn't know till later in life was that they were really a bunch of great guys, they were fun, and they were very friendly. I assumed that they were encouraged to be somewhat stoic during church to set a tone of seriousness. Today, ushers are highly energetic, very courteous and friendly. Within those ushers resided the ability to make people feel welcomed and loved – but it had to be unleashed for people to experience their kindness and humor. Once the church recognized their talent was needed, it was a wonderful transformation. The ushers created a culture of warmth and friendliness and the people reacted extremely positively.

One of the greatest transformations in history was that of baseball legend Mickey Mantle. He grew up in a small town in Missouri, raised by a coal miner, and was such a phenomenal talent that the New York Yankees drafted him right out of high school. Coming from a small town and transitioning to the big city was a major challenge for Mantle. He had difficulty adjusting and considered quitting baseball before his twenty-first birthday. Fortunately for baseball and for the Yankees, Mantle was able to adjust and became one of the greatest baseball players of all time.

Mantle was the darling of every baseball fan and was literally worshipped in New York. The lifestyle of the big city quickly grasped ahold of Mantle and brought out the worst in the young superstar. Mantle, despite being married, began drinking heavily and chasing women. His lifestyle created tremendous tension for his family. I have read many of the books written about Mantle, including his autobiography. He mentions that he was absent from his children's lives, and even once said, "I was a terrible father." The effect of the absent father had a negative impact on his sons. Three of his sons enrolled in the Betty Ford Clinic for alcoholism treatment. Mantle went on to have a tremendous career but frequently said that if he had taken better care of himself he could have been one of the greatest, if not the greatest player of all time.

Late in his life, Mantle also entered the Betty Ford Clinic but the drinking had taken a toll on his body. He was diagnosed with liver failure and despite a transplant, his prognosis was terminal. The transformation that took place in Mantle's life came late but it was better late than never. Mantle spent the last years of his life with his wife and sons trying to be the father and the husband that he had failed to be. He leveraged the strength that had remained hidden within him for years. The Mantle that surfaced transformed from self-centered to selfless, from arrogant to humble, from hard to compassionate and finally from difficult to loving. Before he died, Mantle accepted God into his life and asked forgiveness from his family. One of his former teammates, Bobby Richardson, was instrumental in bringing Mickey Mantle to God. Mantle realized that his greatest strength was his ability to love his family and to ask for forgiveness; not hitting a baseball. It is never too late to leverage your strengths.

Each of you possesses tremendous strengths. To be successful you need to leverage those strengths to accomplish amazing things. People are eager to follow those that demonstrate great qualities. If you have the strength of humility and compassion, leverage that to help others. If your strength is trustworthiness and commanding respect, use it to influence others to the right things. If you have a positive attitude, unleash it on others and make it infectious. If your strength is sacrifice, work relentlessly to help others accomplish greatness. Your strengths are not meant to be kept to yourself, they are meant to change the world. Be aspirational, be a person of influence and be the person others want to follow. You have the strengths, unleash them.

Overcome your weaknesses

Everyone has weaknesses but before you can overcome them you must know what they are, and you must be willing to address them. Weaknesses can be difficult to overcome. It takes a dedicated effort and a support system. If I wanted to get in shape, I would have to change my eating habits and start an exercise program. If I have never done that before it would be painful and take me out of my comfort zone. The end result of getting in shape is that I would feel better and be healthier. It seems logical, but yet every New Year's Day a tremendous number of Americans make a resolution to get in shape then fail to stick with their plan.

Have you had had to change some of your habits? If you did, then you know it is very difficult. There are some bad habits such as smoking and drinking that require immediate attention, because if you do not change you run the risk of losing your health and perhaps suffering permanent damage. Do you know people whose poor habits jeopardize their health? How do you feel when they ignore your advice? It is frustrating when people acknowledge that they have a weakness, they thank you for providing them feedback, and then proceed to do nothing. When these things happen, it is important not to take it personally. Sometimes people have a low drive and struggle to engage in corrective action. Despite your encouragement, they may not be able to push themselves forward. In these situations, assuming they want to change, you should recommend that they seek professional help.

There are many forms of weaknesses that people face today. Here are some examples, and you might know people that are going through these struggles:

- Addiction to alcohol
- Engaging in binge drinking
- Use of drugs
- Poor eating habits
- Lack of exercise
- Smoking
- Texting and driving
- Pornography

These are all damaging behaviors that are damaging and need to be addressed. Though they are weaknesses, they tend to stem from something within the individual that is driving the poor choices. When I talk about weaknesses, I am referring to intangible things in the mental or emotional state. For example, I am not a doctor, but I am convinced that drinking and drugs tend to come from a desire for acceptance. I see that as a weakness. If you were to concentrate on earning the respect of others instead of being liked, you would have an easier time walking away from people that are pushing bad behaviors on you. The same applies to poor eating habits. Many people that fail to eat properly struggle with self-discipline. This can be due to low self-esteem or lack of a positive self-image.

To be successful, you must learn how to overcome weaknesses. The following are some obvious ones:

- Failure to look people in the eye when talking to them
- Failure to greet people
- Displaying rude behavior
- Arrogance
- Failing to follow up on commitments
- Being late
- Lack of integrity
- Disrespectful

Each of these weaknesses is disturbing and will keep you from being successful. It would be impossible to concentrate on all of these at one time. The best way to address a weakness is to isolate it, focus on it, develop a support group to help you, and measure your progress. I do believe that if you focus on a couple of weaknesses it will help with all of them. I would suggest focusing on Treating People with Respect and Becoming a Trustworthy Person. If you struggle with these two, I would highly recommend that you make it a priority to address these immediately. Sometimes the reason we show a lack of respect is because we do not respect ourselves. This requires a serious look in the mirror, and it requires an honest assessment of yourself? Ask yourself some difficult questions that will help you identify the issue.

- Do I like myself?
- Am I proud of how I look?
- Am I proud of how I act?
- Do I have the ability to be successful?
- Do people like me for who I am?

These are tough questions but if you are willing to address your weaknesses, you will experience positive change. Life goes too quickly. Every day is an opportunity to meet people and to make a positive difference in the world. Don't wait for tomorrow to begin your positive journey.

It is difficult to change people's perceptions of you. They have set their minds based on interactions with you or observations they have made. You cannot worry about how people see you. All you can do is to be the best that you can be. By addressing your weaknesses, you will have a positive impact on each new person that comes into your life. It is never too late to start.

It is more useful to be aware of one weakness in yourself than ten thousand in someone else.

Paul overcame his weaknesses and turned them into strengths

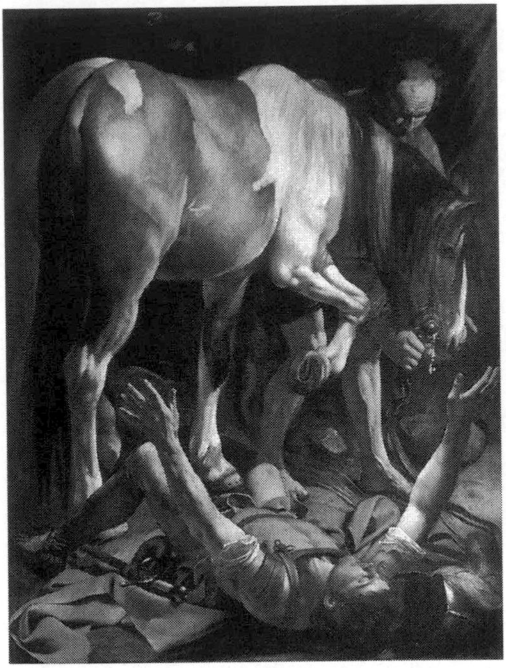

One of the greatest stories of someone who changed and overcame their weaknesses is that of Paul the Apostle. Paul had many weaknesses but his ego, his arrogance and his desire to hurt others were probably his greatest faults.

Paul was a highly educated Roman citizen, may have been a family member of Herod the Great, and was known for his persecution of the followers of Jesus.

As he traveled on the road to Damascus, Paul had an encounter with God – he was struck from his horse and blinded for three days. Paul converted to Christianity, his eyesight was restored, and the experience changed his heart. Paul wrote many of the books in the New Testament and was one of the most influential people in the Bible. Paul preached on three continents and was responsible for spreading Christianity. He was able to overcome his weaknesses by focusing on good works, converting his ego to humility and his anger to compassion.

Paul effectively addressed his weaknesses and became a great role model and leader. Paul became a great defender of the faith, a dynamic and relentless teacher of righteousness, and a fearless preacher to the world. Paul was able to overcome his weaknesses and turn them into strengths. His new and passionate mission created inner strengths in courage, honesty, trustworthiness and tenacity.

What do you see in Paul's story that resemble your challenges? What would it take to convert some of your weaknesses to strength? Are you ready to take the challenge? Each of you has been created for greatness, but you have to be willing to accept the challenge. One of my favorite quotes in the Bible is 2 Timothy, 1:6-7, "For God hath not given us the spirit of fear and timidity; but of power, and of love, and self-discipline." This is a powerful quote and it should embolden you to be courageous and tackle your strengths with pride and optimism.

It is okay to be human

Superman and Wonder Woman are fictional characters. It is important to realize that as humans, you will have ups and downs. You will accomplish great things and you will fail many times. Failing is an important part of growing and learning. As long as you accept failure and learn from the mistakes, you will be okay. All great accomplishments came about through the experience of failure. If you spend time talking to the great inventors, they will tell you that they failed countless times. Great hitters in baseball fail seven out of ten times. You must experience challenges to grow as a person and to build character. How many times have you bombed a test? How many times did you try an experiment before you succeeded? How many great employees have either been fired or have been laid off during their career? Each of these negative experiences has probably taught you great things. It makes you more determined, it builds tenacity, it builds mental toughness and it shows you that failure is not the end of the world.

Of course, all these examples assume that you worked hard something before you failed. If you fail because of lack of preparation, or irresponsible acts, I am not sure what lessons you will absorb, other than not to show poor judgment again. Sometimes we fail because we are overly aggressive, and we take on more than we can handle. Being aggressive and having a high level of initiative is a great thing, but you have to make sure that you don't overcommit to the point where you can't do anything well.

Failure can also be a result of complacency. This can happen if you fail to stay hungry. Complacency can result in others taking your job, your spot on the team, scoring higher in school tests, or in removal from an elected position. Losing a job or losing your starting position due to complacency can be very surprising and disappointing. If this happens or if it has already happened to you, learn from it. Try to understand that there are lots of people that want what you have. If you are not willing to fight hard for it and continue to improve, you can find yourself unseated.

Cockiness or overconfidence is a leading cause of failure. If you study the number of actors that repeatedly turn up as the top actors in Hollywood, you will not find many. The same applies to sports teams. It is very difficult to get to the top and to stay at the top. When you let yourself get too confident you run the risk of not studying enough, not practicing hard, and possibly taking your job for granted. Any of these are dangerous and warrant careful evaluation. I have seen many superstars get beat out by young hungry rookies.

I have also seen many senior executives be replaced in the workplace. Life is very competitive. Bailouts are not the norm, so do not expect one. Every day you have to be at the top of your game.

It is okay to make mistakes. It is important to acknowledge your mistake and take corrective action. Making a mistake should not make you less of a person unless your mistake was deliberate and malicious. In some cases, mistakes make you a greater person. When you are willing to own up to your mistake and you are sincere and honest about it, people will respect you. Have you ever seen Lebron James miss a dunk? Even the greatest basketball player on the planet fails. It is okay to be human.

In the 2012 Republican primary debate, the Governor of Texas, Rick Perry, had a mental lapse and could not remember the answer to a question that he had probably answered many times before. The media ridiculed him and he suffered through the embarrassment. Yet making that mistake did not make Governor Perry less of a person. He handled the issue with grace, and he humbled himself for not remembering the answer to the question. I actually felt terrible for him because I knew that he could have answered the question nine out of ten times. Unfortunately for Governor Perry, he was not able to overcome the blunder in the press. His record as Governor of Texas is remarkable and he did a fantastic job growing the economy.

As he prepared to run for the 2016 presidential election he had to overcome the self-doubt and damage his image took.

We have to continually remind ourselves that we are human. Being human means that we are destined to make mistakes. Either intentional or not, we will make mistakes -- sometimes big ones. Mistakes are part of life and as humans, we have to accept that they will happen. Whether it is the classroom, on the sports fields, in the workplace or your social life, you will do things that you might not be proud of. The key to making a mistake is that you have to be willing to own it. Regardless of the outcome, owning up to a mistake is part of maturity. Owning up to a mistake is not easy but if you do not do it, it will become progressively more difficult to do so.

I used to enjoy the commercial where young boys are playing baseball and they accidentally break a window. Everyone runs except the kid who is holding the bat. The same applies in real life. Instead of everyone owning up to the accident they caused, they hung the one kid out to dry. When you belong to a team and someone messes up, the entire team should own up to it. That is part of stepping up and taking accountability. You will face difficult situations throughout life; how you handle those situations determines your character. Running away from mistakes is common in today's society, but mistakes will eventually catch up to you. By facing up to your mistakes you will develop as a person. Here are some of the benefits of owning up to your mistakes:

- Others will see you as an honest person and it might prove valuable in the future
- It will demonstrate integrity

- It will allow you to learn from the mistake and become stronger
- It will bring respect to you
- It will strengthen relationships with those around you

Remember, it is okay to be human.

Chapter 7 – Believe in Yourself

TO DRIVE TOWARD SUCCESS, you have to believe in yourself. Success requires that you have a clear mission and thorough and realistic goals you want to attain. If you do not have a clear line of sight to what you want to accomplish, how will you know if you are making progress and how will you know when you have attained your goals? Many wonderful ideas are never implemented because the person gave up too soon. They did not believe in themselves or lacked the confidence to keep moving it forward. If you have a clear vision and a passion that burns inside of you to see it through, then you should push hard. Having a passion and a vision is great, but you must be realistic in what you see yourself accomplishing. Some of the questions that you need to ask yourself are as follows:

- Am I dedicated?
- Am I willing to endure criticism?
- Can I overcome my self-doubts?
- Do I have perseverance and stamina?
- Can I influence others to help me?
- Am I willing to see it till the end?
- Am I willing to take the hits and keep getting up?

To believe in yourself is a great quality. It will differentiate you from many others that have the skills, the talent and the ability, but do not have confidence in themselves. Confidence comes from having experienced success in previous ventures, but it also comes from being prepared. If your goal is to be the valedictorian of your school, it requires intense studying, commitment and dedication. It also requires a high degree of intellect. If you are not going to put in the effort, then you should not set being a valedictorian as your goal. The same applies to sports. If you have your heart and soul set on making the starting lineup but you lack the athletic skill to compete at that level, do not make that your goal. I am a firm believer that if you believe in yourself you can aspire to great levels; however, I also believe that you have to be honest with yourself and you have to be realistic.

Let's assume that you have an aspirational goal to cure cancer. Your goal is to work around the clock conducting lab research and your motives are pure. Cancer research has been around for many years, and we have learned that cancer is not just one disease – it takes dozens of different forms that require different types of treatment. If you make curing cancer your aspirational goal, it is highly probable that you will not attain it. Your goals have to be attainable and you have to be able to obtain support from others. If people feel that your goal has zero credibility, you will not get the support needed to move it forward. Believe in yourself, but make sure that you have a solid understanding of what you will need to be successful. Align your goals with your talents and ensure that you have the support system to see them through.

Be proud of who you are

In order to believe in yourself you have to be proud of the person that you are now, and of the person you are aspiring to become. What are the things you are proudest of? Why do you feel this way? It is important to understand what makes you feel proud. If your goal was to get the highest grade in the class and you did, would that make you proud? The obvious answer is yes, but what if you cheated throughout the year and that enabled you to get the highest grade? What if your goal was to win your wrestling match and you did, but you had someone spike the other wrestler's food? You won the match because the other wrestler had to withdraw. These are factors that you have to consider when answering the previous questions.

Be proud of who you are; there is only one of you.

I think being proud of yourself should concentrate on your personal traits instead of your accomplishments. For example, if you attain your goals by working hard, by helping those that need help, and by being selfless, you should be very proud. If you didn't accomplish your goals but you demonstrate all these great traits, you will likely be disappointed about the goals, but you should still be proud of your actions and traits. Being proud should result from what makes you a person, as well as by your accomplishments.

How many people do you know who could drive a fancy car or own a luxurious yacht, but instead, dedicate their lives to helping others? They are generous with their money and use it to help those that need help. They should be very proud of themselves. Believing in yourself is paramount to being successful. The first place to start is for you to be honest with you. If you feel that you are a person of principle, someone who is trustworthy and that commands respect, you should be very proud. Believing in yourself also means that you have to be at peace with yourself. If there is something that is nagging you or tugging at you, it will be difficult to concentrate on your priorities. Do not let things get in your head and distract you from your mission. Be clear on what you are trying to do. Be determined to do it and have a clear mind to steer you in the right direction. If you are distracted or uncomfortable with an action that you have engaged in, avoid making commitments until you can clear up these issues.

People that believe in themselves perform best in the clutch. They understand the nature of the situation and demand to be the "go to" person. When the basketball game is tied and the seconds are counting down, there always seems to be a person that steps up and takes charge. They have ice in their veins and are confident in taking the shot. This is the person that believes in their ability to perform in the clutch.

Do you remember taking part in a big school project? Was there always someone who stepped up to take the lead? That person was confident and believed that he/she would deliver. They understood that the project was very important and that if they stood up, the probability of success was greater.

In the business world, it is critical to have decision makers. There will always be more data and there will always be more opportunities to continue studying what direction to take. The person that believes in himself is the person that says, "We need to act now and move forward." To be that person you must be prepared, you must be confident, and you must be able to deal with the consequences if the decision is flawed.

People that believe in themselves are eager to make the tough decisions. They look for opportunities to make the play when the pressure is on, and they excel in the clutch. Do you believe in yourself? Are you willing to step up? We need great people that are willing to make a difference. Be the person that challenges the norm and has the courage to make the tough decisions. We have too many followers; be a leader!

You never know when a situation is going to require you to make a difficult decision. It can spring up on you and require you to make an immediate decision or it may need to be calculated carefully and requires analysis and guidance from others. There are some tips that might help you in determining how to proceed:

1. Follow the test of the mirror. Will you be able to look in the mirror and know that you acted in the best interest of others and you did the right thing?

2. Think back and assess if you have had to make a similar decision in the past and learn from that previous experience.

3. Assess the pros and cons of your decision.

4. Who will your decision affect, and how?

5. Discuss the situation with trusted people.

6. What will be the expected and unexpected consequences of your decision?

7. Have courage and confidence.

8. Once you make the decision, do not second guess yourself.

It takes courage to live every day. Be strong and proud of yourself. Make each moment count.

Always strive to be better

To enjoy success, it is important that you always aspire to keep growing as a person. There is a saying that goes, "if you stop growing you start dying." I am a big believer that we must continue to challenge ourselves day in and day out. There is always plenty of room for improvement, but we must constantly seek it. Being stagnant is wasting opportunities. There is so much to do in life and so many great causes that need help that you cannot afford to be idle. Have you ever heard stories of senior citizens that go back to school at a late age? It is wonderful that these people have such a thirst for knowledge. Even at an advanced age they want to learn and contribute. As young adults it is imperative that you understand the concept of "striving to get better." Life is very competitive and if you stop improving you will quickly become mediocre. Do you think schools want to recruit mediocre students? Do you think companies want to recruit mediocre workers? How about sports teams? No matter what your talents are, you can always improve. Some say that humans only use between 10-12% of their brains. Imagine what you can accomplish by tapping a little bit more.

Some of the most successful people are those who refuse to become complacent. They keep working on their craft, continuing to find ways to improve their talents. I remember reading about the great basketball player, Kobe Bryant and his insane work ethic. Even at the top of his game, Kobe would practice up to eight hours a day. He was truly inspired to work hard and elevate his game. What people probably do not know is that he plays the piano and speaks seven languages. It is important to elevate all phases of your life. Everyone has great talents that need to be used, do not be afraid to try new things. You might surprise yourself and others.

Great scientists, artists and musicians are noted for their dedication to their field. They will spend countless hours perfecting their talent. We are fortunate to have these great people because we are the beneficiaries of their talent. I have read many stories of coaches that began preparation for the next season the day their season ended. They would not even take one day off. These are the type of individuals that refuse to be complacent. They are driven and they are determined to elevate their talents.

My uncle was one of these, a very talented radiologist. He worked countless hours at Mount Sinai Hospital in Miami Beach, Florida. He dedicated his entire life to helping others and was always in demand, traveling throughout the world to educate others on his craft. He realized that there was a tremendous need for his skills in radiology and was willing to share them. There are many countries that lack the advanced technology that we have here in the United States. He was determined and driven to help others elevate their level of expertise in the medical field. One of the qualities that my uncle possessed was the willingness to take time out of his personal life to take phone calls from people that needed medical help not necessarily related to radiology. People called his house at all times of the night to seek his counsel. I do not ever remember a time when he turned people away and refused to help.

As busy as he was with his medical practice, he also developed a passion for playing the trumpet. He would call me at night to go over to his house and listen to his newfound hobby. As much as I loved my uncle and as much as I enjoyed being with him, the trumpet was not one of his greatest skills. He would butcher some notes and then ask me what I thought. Since I didn't want to hurt his feelings, I would tell him that he was doing great and constantly improving. It was painful to stay there and listen, but I knew that it was his way of relaxing. Here he was at the top of his medical profession and he was determined to master another skill. As I look back, I wish he had taken on a less challenging task. A poor trumpet-playing person can be harmful to your health (lol)! His work ethic and willingness to help others was always an inspiration to me. He helped many but his greatest gift was the knowledge that he passed on to others.

Life is an opportunity to enjoy many different things. Regardless of what you decide to pursue in life, give it your all. Always strive to be the best that you can be and be eager to continue to improve. Always remember that failure is necessary to achieve greatness. Do not get down or become disappointed when you fail; embrace it, learn from it and overcome it. We need people that want to aspire to greatness and make significant contributions. You have many talents that you might not discover until later in life. I would encourage each of you to allow your curiosity to open new opportunities and experiences. Make the most of all of your talents and seek to always learn and grow.

Always be willing to step up

Leaders understand that to be successful they have to be willing to step up. That is what leaders do and if you want to be the best, that is what is expected of you. Stepping up means that when a situation requires an important decision, you show courage and you make that decision. When life requires action, you take it. Stepping up also means that if you see something wrong, you correct it. Imagine that you are walking by the side of the road and you witness an accident. Someone in the car is crying out for help. Leaders step up and help the person in need. There are many things that will differentiate you from the crowd. To be successful you are the one that people expect to step up and make the right decision. Here are a few examples of things that are happening in our country that require immediate attention and are in need of someone stepping up:

- Domestic violence
- Child abuse
- Binge drinking
- Drinking and driving
- Teen violence
- Gangs
- Drug abuse
- Addiction to pornography
- Hate crimes
- Prevalence of filthy language
- Children without fathers
- Animosity towards police officers
- Lack of trust in politicians
- Divisiveness within our country
- Immigration and border control

There are probably other issues that I have left out, but I wanted to provide a feel for issues that are in desperate need of someone stepping up and working towards solutions. Do you know someone that is crying out for help? Is there something that you can do to help out?

Kerri Strug: The Heart of a Warrior

In the 1996 Summer Olympics the United States Women's Gymnastics team was the favorite to win the gold medal. They were in command and the gold medal was in sight. A streak of bad luck hit the team, and many of the gymnasts began to experience difficulty. There was misfortune after misfortune. Gymnast after gymnast fell in their event. With one competitor to go, the medal was in jeopardy. The last event rested on the shoulders of young Kerri Strug: it was the vault and it required a great result. With the crowd on its feet, Strug took a deep breath and sprinted down the 75-foot runway like a woman possessed. She performed a difficult vault with a handspring and a twisting dismount. As she descended through the air toward the ground, she slipped on her landing and fell on her backside. She also heard a snap in her left ankle. There is disbelief in the crowd. The gold, it appears, is gone when Strug's score – 9.162 – is flashed on the board.

Strug fell to her knees, disregarding her injured ankle. Her parents, sitting in the stands, covered their faces. As Strug rose and begins psyching herself up for her second and final vault, pain shot through her leg. She had suffered two torn ligaments in the ankle.

There was chaos on the sidelines. Strug's ankle throbbed badly and her head ached. Her teammates encouraged her. The U.S. coaches looked up at the scoreboard, then over at the Russians performing the floor exercises.

Kerri Strug stepped up and delivered gold

The coaches couldn't compute quickly enough whether Strug even needed to vault a second time on a sprained ankle in order to guarantee the American women the gold medal.[2]

Kerri had a tough decision to make. She had not come this far and trained so hard to quit one vault short of the gold medal. Kerri knew she had a serious injury, but she heard her coach say, "We need you Kerri, you can do it." Kerri nodded and began to line up for the final sprint to the vault. She knew she could not place much pressure on

[2] http://sports.espn.go.com/espn/espn25/story?page=moments/51

the ankle but was determined to make the vault. Amazingly, Kerri found the adrenaline to fly down the runway. She knew she must land flawlessly for the judges.

Kerri hit the vault and flew through the air. With the crowd watching in deep suspense, Kerri flawlessly nails the landing and secures the gold medal. This has to be one of the greatest examples of stepping up. Kerri Strug was a real warrior that night and all Americans should be very proud of her.[3]

Make a difference with your actions

I am a big believer that actions speak a lot louder than words. Many people spend too much time boasting about all the things they are going to accomplish, but never deliver. There are always exceptions, but it seems that the people who spend little to no time talking are the ones that deliver the most results. Successful people do not need to tell you all the great things that they did or are going to do; they just do it. The Nike slogan "Just do it" is a good example of emphasizing actions instead of words. People are interested in results not promises. They navigate towards those with a history of generating positive actions.

If you are investing in a company, would you rather invest in a company that makes great promises but fails to deliver or in a company that has a proven track record? The same will apply when you go searching for the right employer. As a talented young adult, companies will target you for either internships or permanent

---

[3] https://www.youtube.com/watch?v=AlGCfS-F22I

employment. When companies are in the process of recruiting, they tend to make a lot of promises. Always ask them to put their promises in writing. If they fail to do so, it means they are not credible. Successful companies are willing to back up what they say. If you are in a position where a company is making all sorts of promises, ask the company to put it in writing. If they refuse to do so, this is a company you should steer clear of. The same is true of people; they tend to make lots of declarations – look for those who actually do something.

As a young adult you have an opportunity to achieve great things. You want to make sure you focus on your actions. Let your actions create your legacy and reputation. You always want to be known for being the person who delivers in the clutch, the person who comes through when they are needed, the person who is dependable, responsible and accountable, the person who does what he says. If you focus on these principles, you will be someone who makes a difference. If you watch television, you will see all the people who are boasting about all kinds of things. They brag, they make promises and they lead you to believe that they have great importance. These are the people that you need to avoid. You want to associate with those who are humble and soft spoken but accomplish greatness. One of these men is Dr. Ben Carson. He is a true example of the "American Dream."

Dr. Carson was born in Detroit, Michigan. At the age of eight, his parents were divorced, and his mother raised him and his older brother. His mother, a very poor woman, had dropped out of school in the third grade and was married at the age of thirteen. She later found out that her husband was a bigamist and divorced him. Mrs. Carson was financially devastated. To make ends meet, she worked up to three jobs at a time. Because of this difficult schedule, Ben and his brothers were alone quite a bit.

Ben quickly found his way into trouble and suffered from anger issues. He also found himself at the bottom of his school class.

Determined to help her children find their way out of poverty, Mrs. Carson limited the amount of television and had the boys focus on reading books. Despite being barely able to read herself, she would make the boys read two library books a week and pretend to test them. Though Ben initially resisted the reading regimen, he soon began to enjoy reading and made significant improvement in school. Ben ultimately graduated high school with honors. Determined to go to college, he worked in the automotive industry and earned enough money to attend Yale. After graduating from Yale, Ben enrolled at the University of Michigan Medical School and went on to complete his residency at Johns Hopkins University in Baltimore. Ben specialized in neurosurgery and went on to become one of the leading neurosurgeons in the country.

His story is an amazing ride from poverty to success. He accomplished all this with dedication, hard work and perseverance. Fortunately for Americans, Dr. Carson's story is still evolving. He continues to challenge himself and is striving to be better. He has become a successful author and even ran as a Republican candidate for the 2016 presidency. I am convinced that his intellect and analytical capabilities would have been very valuable. Fortunately for all Americans, Dr. Carson was appointed to lead the Department of Housing and Urban Development. Can you imagine, a poor young man with anger issues defying all the odds to run for president? I have had the distinct honor of meeting Dr. Carson. He is a very humble individual who cares deeply about our country. I cannot say enough good things about Dr. Carson, and I know that in everything he has aspired to do, he has accomplished greatness. We are blessed to have him eager to strive to become even better. Dr. Carson's actions have spoken much louder than words could have.

In today's society, we are exposed to many celebrities that like to hear themselves talk, but don't actually say much of value. They are referred to as "talking heads." They can be political analysts, celebrities, athletes or entertainers. They rant and rave and they tend to be self-centered. In many cases they are very condescending and berating to those that oppose their views. These types of individuals can be careless with their words but can also be influential. When I see these types of people, I do not tend to pay too much attention to what they are saying. My preference is to pay attention to people who lead by their actions. They command respect for results, not words.

Stand tall and be proud

Successful people stand tall and are proud. When you make the decision to be a person of integrity and a person that is willing to work hard and aspire to greatness, you also have every right to stand tall and be proud. This requires that your motives for your actions are pure. You also have a desire to help others, especially those that cannot help themselves. It is a great feeling to know that your actions and your behavior are driven by a good cause. You work hard, you go the extra mile, you work through adversity and you ultimately persevere. This is what drives success. You might be thinking there are people who take short cuts or they lie, steal and cheat to get ahead. I am sure that there are many people that engage in behavior that is reckless and irresponsible. But these types of people will not be able to stand tall and to be proud. They will never be able to look in the mirror and be proud of who they are. They might be temporarily successful, but they will ultimately become a failure. They are deceiving others, but more importantly, they are deceiving themselves.

As a young adult it is important to understand how you define a successful person. Many people are identified as successful solely because they have made (or inherited) money. This is probably the shallowest way of identifying success, but success constitutes many intangible aspects. Here are some factors that you should consider when labeling someone a success:

- Are they a good person?
- Do they treat others with respect?
- Are they trustworthy?
- Are they a good parent?
- Are they a good spouse?
- Are they willing to help others?

- Are they a person of integrity?
- Are they self-centered or selfless?
- Do they take advantage of others?
- Do they sacrifice for their organization?
- Do they sacrifice for their family?
- Have they taken advantage of others or have they earned their success?
- Are they ethical?
- Do they stand tall and proud?

These are important questions that you should consider when someone mentions the term, "Successful Person."

Heather Whitestone is a person I respect and admire. Heather was born in Alabama in 1973 and at the age of eighteen months was diagnosed as being deaf. Despite her physical disability, Heather was crowned Miss America in 1995. As a child, Heather developed a passion for ballet, even though she could not hear the music. She worked diligently on her ballet talents and became quite good at it. Earning the Miss America crown was an amazing feat. Heather had to deal with the physical, emotional and mental challenges of her physical disability. During the pageant, Heather was able to showcase her S.T.A.R.S. program, which stands for "Success Through Action and Realization of your dreams." It has five points which are: positive attitude, belief in a dream, the willingness to work hard, facing obstacles, and building a strong support team. Heather has authored four books and does motivational speaking across the nation. She has refused to let her disability hold her back. Heather is an amazing woman who has a close relationship with God. She has refused to rest on her laurels; instead, she is actively serving others in many capacities. Her accomplishments include:

- Appointed by President Bush and confirmed by the U.S. Senate to the National Council on Disability - Resigned in 2010.

- Becoming a board member for the Helen Keller Foundation for Research and Education, from 1995-2002.

- She was appointed to the Advisory Council for the National Institute of Health on Deafness and Other Communication Disorders, in 2002.

- In 2003, she filmed two public service announcements to bring awareness about Dogs for the Deaf, a hearing-dog organization.

She became a spokesperson for the Starkey Hearing Aid Foundation and for Cochlear America's. She has also spearheaded the nation's largest multimedia public service campaign to identify early hearing loss, created by the Miss America Organization and the

Alexander Graham Bell Association for the Deaf. Heather is a tremendous role model and exemplifies the meaning of success. She stands tall and proud.

To stand tall and be proud requires you to make tough decisions. It will challenge your moral compass and require you to make the choices that earn you respect instead of the choices that make you popular. Regardless of whether you are active in sports, in school or in the workplace, there are issues that will confront you every day. Let me paint a picture of situations that could arise in each of these three areas:

Sports: Over the last two decades we have seen an increasing pressure to win at all costs. This pressure has resulted in some individuals and organizations to make poor decisions and pursue irresponsible behaviors. One of the most prevalent issues in sports is the use of performance enhancing drugs. PEP's are typically steroids and growth hormones; however, there are also instances where players use prescription drugs for Attention Deficit Disorder or for inflammation/pain killers. The dangers of using these drugs have been documented by the medical profession. Not only do you risk personal health problems but you also risk being suspended or even banned from the sport. Ultimately, the use of illegal drugs will result in your reputation being tarnished and you will suffer a black eye in the public domain. It is important to ask yourself if it is really worth endangering your life and is it worth having to look at children that have rooted for you and called you their role model and tell them that you cheated. Sports as a profession is difficult and the competition is intense. If you want to stand tall and be proud, make the right choices.

School: As young adults you are faced with tremendous pressure in school and from society. The competition to do well and to be accepted into college or the workplace has intensified through the years. This phenomenon has caused some students to revert to stealing, lying and cheating. You will also face the pressure of drinking and engaging in drugs. These are temptations that you must avoid. Nothing positive will ever come from drinking or drugs and I would challenge anyone and everyone that differs. To be successful, you need to avoid behaviors that will jeopardize you from achieving greatness. There are numerous stories of individuals that did not exercise sound judgment or failed to demonstrate the courage to stand up to irresponsible behaviors. Unfortunately, in many cases their future was adversely affected. Stand tall and be proud by saying no to things that will hurt you.

Workplace: In the workplace there is also intense competition both at the personal level and at the organization level. One of the most talked about issues today is hacking. This is the practice of breaking into someone's personal information or an organization's proprietary business information to steal confidential data. This type of theft is also being conducted every day by foreign governments. This is unethical and illegal. Regardless of the intense pressure to compete, you need to refrain from conduct that is wrong. In the workplace there is also temptation to take credit for other people's work product. You need to remember that if you are a member of an organization, all the members are playing for the same team. Always take the high road and do the right thing; it should be your only option.

As a young adult you have your entire future ahead of you. Making the right choices will allow you to be successful and keep you in the proper lanes. The impact of making the wrong choices can be devastating and could cost you your future. Be the person who stands tall and is proud to make the right decisions.

Sources

All photos by Student ACES unless otherwise noted.

Baltimore Riot: Bishop M. Cromartie

Winston Churchill: By BiblioArchives / LibraryArchives - https://www.flickr.com/photos/28853433@N02/19086236948/, Public Domain, https://commons.wikimedia.org/w/index.php?curid=41991931

Franklin Graham: Courtesy of Samaritan's Purse International Relief

Melissa Stockwell: By The U.S. Army - Paralympic military sports camp, Public Domain, https://commons.wikimedia.org/w/index.php?curid=22656978

Marriage: Image by 이리나 김 from Pixabay

Army-Navy Game: PHILADELPHIA (Dec. 6, 2008) President George W. Bush conducts the ceremonial coin toss before the start of the 109th Army-Navy college football game at Lincoln Financial Field in Philadelphia. U.S. Navy photo by Mass Communication Specialist 2nd Class Tommy Gilligan/Released

Michael J. Fox: By photo by Alan Light, CC BY 2.0, https://commons.wikimedia.org/w/index.php?curid=1566227

Stevie Wonder: By Qqqqqq at English Wikipedia, CC BY-SA 3.0, https://commons.wikimedia.org/w/index.php?curid=53703970

Serena Williams: By Edwin Martinez from The Bronx - US Open 2013 Part 2 462Uploaded by Flickrworker, CC BY 2.0, https://commons.wikimedia.org/w/index.php?curid=28397227

"Together on the Street" Homeless Man with Dog and Cats: Mike McBey, CC by 2.0

Girl playing with big dog: Image by Steffen L. from Pixabay; no attribution required.

Condoleeza Rice visits Marine Base. Photo is in the Public Domain. U.S. Marine Corps photo by Lance Cpl. Jerry Murphy/Released http://www.marines.mil/unit/basecamppendleton/PublishingImages/2007/070523-m-0582m-rice2.jpg

"Indy Honor Flight": Angela N., CC BY 2.0

Reputation Balloon: chapmanlam_cm, CC BY-SA 2.0

Queen Latifah: By Anthony Quintano from Honolulu, HI, United States - Super Bowl 44 Queen Latifah God Bless America, CC BY 2.0, https://commons.wikimedia.org/w/index.php?curid=56323269

Bobby Bowden: By cholder68 - https://www.flickr.com/photos/cholder68/290264389/, CC BY 2.0, https://commons.wikimedia.org/w/index.php?curid=1369604

Civil War soldiers and chaplain: Library of Congress. Public domain.

Refugees from Cuba arriving in Florida: Historical Museum of Southern Florida.

Malala Yousafzai: By DFID - UK Department for International Development - Malala Yousafzai: Education for girls, CC BY 2.0, https://commons.wikimedia.org/w/index.php?curid=44577822

U.S. Navy SEAL Team: By U.S. Navy photo by Photographer's Mate 2nd Class Michael J. Pusnik, Jr. - http://www.navy.mil/management/photodb/photos/030524-N-

4441P-089.jpg, Public Domain, https://commons.wikimedia.org/w/index.php?curid=7138807

9-11 First Responders memorial: Rebecca Wilson, CC BY 2.0

Soldier helping child: By Sfc. Larry Johns (U.S. Army) - U.S. Department of Defense, Public Domain, https://commons.wikimedia.org/w/index.php?curid=3737038

Ernie Johnson Jr. and Cal Ripken: Keith Allison, CC by SA 2.0.

Church Shooting, Charleston, SC: By Nomader - Own work, CC BY-SA 3.0, https://commons.wikimedia.org/w/index.php?curid=41087950

George W. Bush Warrior 100K: Maj. Randall Stillinger, Public Domain, https://www.dvidshub.net/image/1909347/president-bush-hosts-wounded-service-members-mountain-bike-ride

Challenger STS-51-L crew: NASA, Public domain.

Scrooge: Illustration by Arthur Rackham. Public domain.

Mickey Mantle: By New York Yankees - Heritage Auctions, Public Domain, https://commons.wikimedia.org/w/index.php?curid=42006797

Paul the Apostle: Conversion on the Way to Damascus-Caravaggio (c.1600-1).jpg, Public domain.

Gold Medal Winner: Image by skeeze from Pixabay

Dr. Ben Carson: By United States Department of Housing and Urban Development - https://mobile.twitter.com/SecretaryCarson/photo, Public Domain, https://commons.wikimedia.org/w/index.php?curid=58336352

Heather Whitestone: By Ballerina224 - Own work, CC BY-SA 3.0, https://commons.wikimedia.org/w/index.php?curid=20218991

About Buck Martinez

Buck Martinez is the co-founder of Student ACES for Leadership and a former a corporate executive in the energy industry for over 30 years.

In 2013, Buck and his daughter Krissy Webb launched a non-profit organization, Student ACES, to provide leadership training, mentoring and internships for high school students. Buck has always been involved with students. He has coached many youth sports teams, mentored young men, and has participated in numerous speaking engagements on the topics of youth leadership at universities throughout Florida.

As an energy executive, Buck was responsible for a diverse number of functions, including generation development, labor relations, and strategic planning. He is a nationally acclaimed speaker on Clean Energy.

While in college, Buck was the captain of the baseball team from his sophomore through senior seasons. He received numerous honors but is most proud of the Scholar Athlete Award.

He has a bachelor's degree from St. Thomas University, where he was inducted into the sports Hall of Fame, and an MBA from Nova Southeastern University. He is a graduate of the Boston University Leadership Program, and a member of the Lifeworks Leadership

2014 class. Buck also serves as an adjunct professor at Keiser University.

Buck is also the founder and president of ACE Leadership Group, an organization dedicated to consulting on Character Education, Leadership and Values. He mentors corporate executives and athletes, and helps deploy Leadership and Character programs at universities, and private and public organizations.

Buck resides in Palm Beach Gardens, Florida, with his wife of over 39 years, three daughters and four grandchildren.

About Student ACES

ATHLETICS • COMMUNITY • EDUCATION

Student ACES (ACE) is a 501(c)3 organization dedicated to providing leadership programs, mentoring, scholarships and internship opportunities for high school students. ACE's focus is to inspire, train and mentor a community of Student ACES who exemplify leadership traits in athletics, community service and education. Student ACES is headquartered in Palm Beach Gardens, Florida. A voluntary Board of Directors and a voluntary Advisory Committee manage the organization. ACE relies on a volunteer network of community, state and national leaders to deploy the organization's strategy.

Our Mission: To inspire and develop men and women of character, honor and integrity.

Guiding Principles: We focus on developing each student's leadership capabilities through Athletics, Community and Education. To ensure success, we work closely with our partner high schools to identify students with the initiative, determination and judgment to become tomorrow's leaders. We ensure that our Board of Directors, Advisory Committee and staff members possess the highest standards of ethics, integrity and character. Our motto is "It's all about the students."

Our Approach: The ACE approach is designed to provide students the best opportunities for success. ACE works directly with schools, the local community, and the private sector to create state of the art leadership courses, delivered locally. ACE also works with other charitable organizations to provide our students with real life experiences in management, teamwork, and leadership. ACE works with the local business community to assist ACE Scholars in securing valuable internship opportunities.

Student Selection Process: ACE considers many criteria in determining which students will be selected for invitation into the program. Just as a parent teaches a child behavior and the educator reinforces and models good behavior at school, ACE strives to recognize, inspire and enforce the positive and aspirational characteristics, traits, and behaviors essential for leadership development. By including Athletics and Community in our program, ACE can assess a student's progress as a leader in real time.

We encourage each of the high schools we work with to establish nominating committees to identify the most deserving students. ACE Students are held to a high standard on the athletic field, in the classroom, and in their communities. As leaders, they are expected to demonstrate teamwork, high work ethic, and a willingness to strive to help others.

Leadership development is measured by the student's growing ability to command respect, earn trust, sacrifice for others, and his or her willingness to work hard.

Education: Education is one of the three critical aspects of ACE. The value of an education is priceless and should be encouraged at all levels, and throughout life. At ACE, we encourage our students to work to their fullest potential in the classroom and demonstrate the principles of hard work, teamwork, a desire to help others, and to always exemplify honesty and integrity.

ACE provides mentoring to ACE Scholars when they advance to college. Our expectation is that ACE Scholars will dedicate themselves to being the best that they can be in all aspects of their lives. A good education will provide the building blocks for their foundation.

As ACE Scholars progress through college and graduation, they are expected, as developing leaders, to mentor and coach the next generation of ACE Scholars.

Student Aces for Leadership

Web: www.studentacesforleadership.com

Twitter: @StudentACES

Facebook: www.facebook.com/studentacesforleadership

Email: info@studentacesforleadership.com

Made in the USA
Columbia, SC
19 April 2020

91623188R00135